Bernard McNally

Soldiers and sailors of New Jersey in the Spanish-American War

Embracing a chronological account of the Army and Navy

Bernard McNally

Soldiers and sailors of New Jersey in the Spanish-American War
Embracing a chronological account of the Army and Navy

ISBN/EAN: 9783337136079

Printed in Europe, USA, Canada, Australia, Japan

Cover: Foto ©ninafisch / pixelio.de

More available books at **www.hansebooks.com**

SOLDIERS AND SAILORS

OF NEW JERSEY

IN THE

SPANISH - AMERICAN WAR,

EMBRACING A

CHRONOLOGICAL ACCOUNT

OF THE

ARMY AND NAVY.

PUBLISHER,
B McNALLY,
NEWARK, N. J.

F
853
54

McNally, Bernard, *comp.*

Soldiers and sailors of New Jersey in the Spanish-American war, embracing a chronological account of the army and navy. Newark, N. J., B. McNally, ᶜ1898.

46 p. 26ᶜᵐ.

Includes a history and roster of the First regiment of New Jersey volunteer infantry, 1898.

1. New Jersey—Hist.—War of 1898. 2. U. S.—Hist.—War of 1898—N. J. inf.—1st. 3. New Jersey infantry. 1st regt., 1898. ɪ. Title.

1-27846 Revised

PREFACE.

In presenting the essential incidents of the opposing forces in the late war between United States and Spain, and from which such vast results have come to this country, we have deemed it sufficient in a work of this character to present the facts briefly in their sequences, and in chronological form. I have begun with the ordering by our government of the U. S. battleship Maine to the harbor of Havana, January 25th, 1898. From that date the acts of the contending powers have been chronicled down through the past eight months, showing the operations of the civil, the armies and navies of the respective contending governments.

After the prominent acts of the general government engaged in the late war have been stated, I have devoted a liberal space to the action of the State of New Jersey and its executive authority relating to war affairs. In this part of the work I have given all the facts of interest relating to the formation of the First Regiment N. J. Volunteers, and the mustering of it into the United States service; the departure of the same from Newark to Camp Voorhees at Sea Girt, N. J., and also its departure from New Jersey to camp life in Virginia, and its final return home. In naval affairs I have given a pretty full history of the New Jersey Naval Reserves, and an extended account of the cruising and other duties of the U. S. S. Badger. These two accounts have been kindly furnished for the work—"Soldiers and Sailors of New Jersey " in the Spanish-American war, by Lieut. Thomas Goldingay of the Badger. For other facts and assistance I am indebted to Mr Charles S. Allen, the war correspondent from the different camps of the First Regiment N. J. Volunteers, to the Newark Daily Advertiser.

For facts relating to Co. G, First Regiment N. Volunteers, and those who enlisted in other companies and in other military organizations, and in the naval branch of the United States service, and the facts and incidents, showing the action of the citizens of Harrison, Kearny, Arlington, and the Borough of East Newark in their relation to the soldiers and sailors who enlisted in the war, from those towns and boroughs, I hereby acknowledge the services rendered me by Mr. William G. Greenfield, President of the Board of Education, Kearny, N. J., and Mr. James Reilly, Assistant, of the Board of Trade, of Newark. Last, though not least in the preparation of these pages, I have had the assistance of a painstaking and arduous labor of Mr. James D. Booraem, of this city.

In these pages no attempt has been made at criticism or deductions or quivering; finally drawing conclusions, all of this has been passed over. The compiler claims no further merit than the facts arranged along these pages may serve the purpose of guiding and stimulating others to undertake elaborate work on this subject, as a fingerboard does sometimes when placed at crossroads, points out and tells the traveler which is the shortest and best way to reach the goal.

B. McNALLY, Publisher.

October, 1898.

BRIEF HISTORY OF THE
Naval Reserves of New Jersey.

The naval militia of the several States is about twelve thousand strong, and is rapidly growing in numbers and increasing in efficiency. Of the total, New Jersey has about 400. The naval militia organization in this State is known as the Naval Reserve of New Jersey. It is divided into the Battalion of the East and the Battalion of the West. The Battalion of the East has for its headquarters the sloop-of-war Portsmouth, at present lying at the foot of Fifteenth Street, Hoboken; it is commanded by Lieutenant Commander Washington Irving. To the Battalion of the West has been assigned as headquarters and training-ship the Monitor Ajax, now docked in Camden. This battalion has for its chief officer Commander Dahlgren.

The scope of usefulness of the naval militia has never been defined with exactness. Generally speaking, the object of organizing it was to supply the United States Navy with a reserve force of trained men to be called upon in case of war. As the several States having naval militia organizations bear nearly all of the cost of their maintenance, those organizations are expected also to co-operate with the National Guard in the event of domestic disturbance. Their training, however, is entirely on naval lines, its direct aim being to render each such organization as one of the New Jersey battalions able to man and work a fighting ship without assistance from the regulars.

The first official sanction given by this State to the establishment of a naval militia was embodied in an enactment of the Legislature of 1894, which was never acted upon by the State military authorities, because of certain defects which it contained. Previous to the passage of this law a battalion of naval militia had been formed in Jersey City and it was through its efforts that the law was passed. It was modelled on the plan of the First Naval Battalion of New York. As a civil organization the rank of commander was conferred upon Edward McClure Peters, as a token of appreciation of his assistance to the young organization.

The members held meetings in Company A's headquarters in the old Fourth Regiment Armory and Captain Keim drilled them. Mainly through the writings of Frank J. Urquhart in the "Newark Sunday Call," interest in the naval militia was aroused in Newark, and the muster-roll of the Jersey City battalion soon began to show Newark names. In August, 1894, the Newarkers became so numerous in the organization that they asked leave to form themselves into a separate division of the battalion, with headquarters in Newark. Permission was granted them, and on the first Monday evening of September they organized in Chosen Friends' Hall, at the corner of Market and Broad Streets, Newark.

In January, 1895, the dissolution of the provisional organization seemed imminent when the Second Division took the administration of affairs into its own hands. It opened up communications with the provisional Battalion of the West, proposed that the Governor should be asked why the men were not mustered in, and that if a defect in the law were the cause it should be remedied at once. A committee, consisting of Lieutenant Urquhart, Ensign Prieth and Boatswain's Mate Tansey, called upon the Governor, discovered that the law was defective, and drafted a new bill, which the members of the Battalion of the West put before the Legislature. It was passed and is the present law.

Interest revived sufficiently after the passage of this law to enable the division to hold together the members it then had. On May 20, 1895, they assembled in Ferryman's Hall, Hoboken, and were mustered in by Lieutenant-Commander Washington Irving, who had been appointed a short time before to organize the Battalion of the East. Captain Jaques was present and made an address to the recruits. The Jersey City Division was first mustered in. It was named the First Division, and the Newark Division was called the Second.

On June 29, 1895, the Portsmouth was brought from the Navy Yard to 14th St.

Hoboken, and was put into commission on August 24, with proper ceremonies. Lieutenant-Commander Irving announced on that day the appointment of Lieutenant Edward M. C. Peters as Navigator, Lieutenant Farnham Yardley as Adjutant, and Lieutenant Arthur H. Colby as Paymaster.

The battalion went into camp at Boynton Beach on August 31, 1895, after having made the journey to that place in the ship's boat. On the way a fierce storm was encountered, giving the men an opportunity to display their pluck and endurance, which they did so well as to bring words of praise from the Lieutenant-Commander.

The 3d Division of Engineers was added to the Battalion in November, '98, and was made up chiefly from students of Stevens Institute, Hoboken.

During the Winter of '95-'96 they were drilled on the Portsmouth and in different halls which they hired at their own expense, in artillery, infantry and learned the rudiments of seamanship.

On July 26th the Battalion of the East put to sea in the Portsmouth, and made a week's voyage on Long Island Sound, entirely manning and handling her. (be it remembered that she is a sailing ship.)

In the Winter of '96 and '97, drills were resumed as in the previous year under the same disadvantages. Many legislative attempts were made during February, '96, to put the organization out of existence, but they failed.

In May, '97, the Reserves paraded at Washington at the inauguration of President McKinley.

On July 27, '97, the Reserves sailed away again on their annual cruise, a more extended one than the previous year, as they sailed up Long Island Sound, to the Capes of Delaware and home, occupying a little over two weeks. During the cruise three days were spent on board the U. S. S. Maine, at heavy gun drill.

In the Winter of '97-'98, drills were again resumed, and legislative attempts to disband the Reserves again made their appearance without success.

During the season maps were made of the river Passaic, and its approaches, by members of the Second Division.

At the outbreak of the war the Reserves immediately offered their services to the Government and the offer was accepted. They were ordered to man the U. S. S. Badger, which they did, fully manning her and serving in her through the late war.

THE U. S. S. PORTSMOUTH.

Home and Training Ship of the New Jersey Naval Reserve.

The United States Sloop-of-War Portsmouth is of 1,000 tonnage and 151 feet long. She was launched at Kittery, Maine, in 1843, and was one of the staunchest and fastest vessels of her class ever built.

In an article written by Rear Admiral Edward Sampson, U. S. N., entitled, "The United States Navy In Transition," which appeared in "Harper's Magazine" of June, 1886, are the following sentences: "Our wooden ships that sailed the ocean from 1840 to 1860 were the finest in the world. The old frigate Congress in 1842 was the noblest specimen of the frigates of the day, and the sloop-of-war Portsmouth was unsurpassed as a corvette; these ships need no eulogy beyond their own record, and were models for the imitation of all maritime nations."

The Portsmouth carried a heavy battery of 22 guns, 6 long twenty-eights, and sixteen long twenty-twos. Her crew, officers and men numbered about 260.

Her first service was done in the Mexican war. She was cruising in the Pacific off the coast of California when she encountered the big frigate Admittance, which was in the service of the Mexican government. Size of battery was greatly in favor of the Mexican, but after an hour's hard fighting she struck her colors to the little Portsmouth, and was towed into port a very sorry looking wreck.

Shortly after that she and the Congress bombarded Guaymas, on the Gulf of California, and after a fierce fight captured it. That night, as the victorious vessel lay at anchor in the harbor, the brigantine Argo, whose captain was unaware of her presence there sailed in. A lieutenant, two midshipmen and a few sailors from the Portsmouth boarded her silently, and the Argo was captured without striking a blow.

In the two years following the Portsmouth further embellished her career by taking many prizes along the Mexican coast.

In 1848 she sailed for Africa and became the flagship of Commodore Gregory. It was while on this station she won her laurels as a fast sailer, chasing and capturing many speedy slave ships.

She next went to Japan, in Commodore Perry's fleet, when he negotiated the treaty opening up the ports of that country to American trade.

From 1856 to 1858 she was in charge of Commodore Foote, and in that time travelled 40,000 miles. The bombardment and destruction of the Barrier Forts below Canton, China, which occurred in September, 1856, was caused by the Chinese firing upon the American flag carried by a cutter from the Portsmouth. This insult was not carried to Washington to be diplomatically attended to and wiped out by an apology. The fleet, consisting of the Portsmouth, San Jacinto and Levant, immediately opened fire on the forts, and after nearly two days' hard fighting captured the forts and 170 guns. The Barrier Forts were previous to this considered impregnable. The Portsmouth was in the thickest of the fighting all through the bombardment, and for the destruction she wrought was christened the "Black Devil."

At the beginning of the Civil War the Portsmouth was sent with Farragut's fleet below New Orleans, and was later made Admiral Porter's flagship. She was in the midst of the mortar flotilla, which was screened with branches of trees lashed to the masts of rigging to deceive the night sentinels at Forts Jackson and St. Philip, when the attempt to pass the forts was made. The attempt was discovered, however, and as the batteries thundered from the forts, the Portsmouth opened up in reply, but the line by which the steamer towed her was severed, and for a time she seemed to be at the mercy of the enemy's guns, but she made sail and escaped, and ever since she is believed by sailormen to bear a charmed existence.

Since the war she has had a more peaceful time, and during the last few years has been used as a school ship, from which thousands of Uncle Sam's sailors have graduated.

The Portsmouth came into the possession of the New Jersey Naval Reserve in August, 1895, and very proud the Reserves are of her.

THE U. S. AUXILIARY CRUISER BADGER.

Which was fully manned by the New Jersey Naval Reserves during the past war with Spain.

The U. S. S. Badger was purchased at the outbreak of the war from the New York and Cuba Mail and Transportation Co., better known, probably, as the "Ward Line." She was formerly known as the "Yumuri," was launched at Roach's shipyard, Chester, Pa., in 1889, and up to the time of her purchase by the Government has been running between New York, Havana and Vera Cruz as passenger and mail steamer.

She is about 3,300 tonnage, is 326 feet long and 43 feet beam, draws about 18 feet of water, is capable of a speed of 15 knots, and can carry about 1,300 tons of coal.

She was altered into an auxiliary cruiser by the Morgan Iron Works at the foot of 9th St., New York, and her armament, consisting of 6 five-inch breech loading guns of the latest pattern, and 6 three-pounder Maxim Nordenfeldt semi-automatic guns, was placed. She was put in commission on May 2, 1898, with Commander A. S. Snow commanding, and twelve days later the Governor of New Jersey was ordered to man her from the Battalion of the East, New Jersey Naval Reserves.

ROUGH LOG OF THE U. S. S. BADGER DURING THE LATE WAR WITH SPAIN.

1898.

May 17. After more than three weeks of expectancy, anxiety and a desire to be of service to their country, the N. J. Naval Reserves, Battalion of the East, were ordered to report on board the U. S. S. Portsmouth, to be examined as to their fitness to serve Uncle Sam, and were officially notified that they were to man the U. S. S. Badger, which was nearly ready.

18. The men of the three divisions reported on board the Portsmouth, and were examined by Assistant Surgeon Pickerell of

the U. S. Navy; this work occupied nearly seven days.

21. The men who were passed by the Surgeon were mustered into the U. S. service for one year, or until the expiration of the war, by Lieutenant D. A. Mahan, of the U. S. N., who is appointed the Executive Officer of the Badger. The officers of the N. J. Naval Reserve, who have been appointed to the Badger, received their commission from the President.

24 to 28. Was occupied in thoroughly equipping the men with clothing, giving them the Badger stations, and also in giving them liberty to say good-bye to their relatives and friends.

29. Sunday—Everything is ready now to go aboard the Badger, and at 12 o'clock when the Navy Yard tug Narkeeta comes alongside the Portsmouth, the bags and hammocks are transferred, and then the N. J. Naval Reserves, amid the cheering of thousands of their friends ashore, board the tug for their new ship. On their way around to 9th Street, they receive a very noisy demonstration in the way of cheering and steam whistles from vessels lying in the harbor cleaning ship.

30. Was occupied in cleaning ship.

31. Got up steam and moved over to Navy Yard at the Cob Dock.

June 1 to 6. Was occupied in getting aboard ordnance stores, equipment stores, ammunition, provisions and coal—five very busy days.

7. Off to Sea—At 10:30 a. m. the lines were cast off and the Badger headed down East River with sealed orders. Passing under Brooklyn Bridge the crew were mustered at quarters; passed Sandy Hook Lightship at 1:30 and course was made E S E after dropping the pilot.

8. At 2:45 a. m. the Badger, which was running without sidelights, came across another vessel which had no running lights out, but put up two white lights when about 400 yards distant. The Badger's crew were instantly called to general quarters and the guns loaded, signals were made, but not answered, and it was thought she was a Spanish man of war. Three shots were fired at the stranger, but a heavy fog coming on, the vessels were lost to each other. At 9 o'clock a. m., all hands were called to general quarters again, whilst off Nantucket shoal light, when a number of strange vessels were seen. Dropped anchor in Provincetown, Mass., at 10:00 p. m.

9 to 10. At anchor in Provincetown. Crew at exercises at quarters and at target practice. Lieut. Mahan was sent to Boston hospital.

10 to 22. The Badger was engaged during these days in patrolling the coast from Segum Light to the Grand Manan, being nearly every night at sea without any lights of any kind, and looking for the Spanish fleet, which was supposed to be laying around the New England coast. On June 18th the Badger rode out a very heavy gale. During these days there was drill—drill—drill, everything from lashing a hammock to clear ship for action. Target practice nearly all the time; everything being done to get the ship in fighting trim.

22 to 25. Badger goes to Portland and commences to coal ship immediately after anchoring; four days of very hard dirty work for men who are not used to it, but done with a good will, for there are rumors that the Badger is going South soon; on the 25th the Badger captures her first prize, a dory that was adrift.

26 to July 1. Hurrah! The Badger is ordered to Key West, and the men finish the coaling in the same spirit they would play foot ball; everybody is full of enthusiasm. They are going to the front at last, hurrah! Got underway at 9 o'clock and proceed South in pleasant weather, with few incidents other than holding up all the ships they pass, and

making them show their colors; meeting the San Francisco and the Prairie on the way down.

July. 1. Arrived in Key West and found the weather very hot and entirely different to what it had been North; took on some stores and mail for the fleet on July 3d; left Key West with orders for Havana; arriving off Morro Castle at daybreak on July 4th, was given her station on the blockading squadron and settled down to business. In the afternoon there were games and singing by the crew in celebration of the glorious 4th.

5. Off Havana—At daybreak a strange vessel was observed which went to sea again, and later was picked up by the Hawk and run ashore off Mariel; when the firing commenced the Badger and Prairie went to the aid of the Hawk, and the vessel which afterwards proved to be the Alphonso XII, was set on fire by the shells exploding in her.

6. Off Havana—Firing heard again in the direction of Mariel. Cleared the ship for action and was put full speed ahead for the scene of action, followed by the Prairie. The Castine was found engaged with two sand forts at the entrance of Mariel harbor. The engagement was a short one, lasting only about an hour, with little satisfaction, as the forts being masked, it could not be told if much damage was done.

7. Off Havana—Badger still off Havana, and ran in close enough to-day to see the heavy batteries ashore; had target practice, and in the afternoon the boys were catching sharks, which are very numerous. The lighthouse off Morro Castle was put out for about three hours, which causes a good deal of work on board the ships of the blockading squadron, who, having no bearing to guide them, got off their stations, and were heaving each other to, thinking they were blockade runners.

8. Off Havana—About noon to-day a vessel was reported making for Havana. The Badger's crew were called to quarters, and the chase began. The stranger was made out to be a man of war, but displayed no colors; she was overhauled in about an hour and hove to with a blank shot, when she hoisted the French flag and reported herself as the Frigate D'Estaing. She was ordered to report to the flag ship, which she did, no doubt convinced that the blockade of Havana was all right. At night the searchlight on Morro Castle was showing up all the ships of the squadron, probably intending to guide blockade runners. First news of the destruction of Cervera's fleet was brought to the Badger to-day by the Hawk, and occasioned a very noisy celebration after the boys went down to supper.

9. Havana—Saturday and general cleaning day with an inspection of clothing and hammocks in the forenoon.

10. Havana—About 10 a. m., just as the men of the Badger were ready for inspection, firing was heard down at Mariel; Badger cleared ship for action and headed for where the firing was going on, followed by two other ships of the squadron, much to the disgust of the boys; they arrived only in time to see the wind up of an engagement between the San Francisco and the sand batteries.

11. Badger was ordered to proceed to Nuevitas to blockade the port; the run of 300 miles was made without accident, other than stopping at Cardenas. Badger arrived off Nuevitas about 5 p. m. of the 12th, and a half hour later chased a steamer which proved to be the U. S. S. Topeka.

13. Nuevitas—At about 2:40 a. m. chased a steamer which proved to be an Austrian man of war; she decorated herself with colors and brought lights; she had no doubt, been held up many times previously.

14. Tug Hudson passed to westward during the night, and had strong easterly winds with heavy sea running.
15. Squally, with heavy sea; drinking water is 85 degrees, and grub is getting down to hard pan.
16. Fires were seen all around Nuevitas during the evening; probably plantations being burned by the Cubans.
17. Spoke to the San Francisco in the morning, and afterward chased and hove to a schooner flying the British flag, with a Spanish crew on board. She was warned of the blockade and let go. At 11 p. m. a steamer light was picked up close inshore, and was hove to. She proved to be the Newfoundland, a British ship, and was boarded and warned of the blockade.
18. At 6 a. m. the Badger had a long chase after a small steamer, which hove to after having five 5-inch shells sent after her at five miles range. She turned out to be the Three Friends, of filibustering fame; she was let go after being warned.
19 and 20. Nothing of importance occurred; searching the sea.
21. Picked up small sloop with four refugees.
22. Saw four of our ships going to eastward, probably to Porto Rico (Amphathrite, Puritan, Montgomery and Supply.)
23. Picked up small sloop with 22 refugees, who reported that Jibara had surrendered to the Prairie. Had a fine concert in the evening on board.
24. Seven Spanish soldiers surrendered to Badger with their arms and ammunition; large schooner came out of Nuevitas with about 70 refugees on board, who wanted to go to Nassau, N. P.; they were allowed to proceed. The Badger men are hoping to go in and capture Nuevitas.
25. Hove to a schooner, the Belencita, of Nassau, N. P., with defaced papers; she was, however, let go after being warned. Another Spanish soldier surrendered to Badger. Nuevitas is being evacuated to-day; about 4,000 Spanish soldiers have gone to Holguin.
26. At 3:45 p. m. a steamer towing two sailing vessels came out of Nuevitas; ship was cleared for action as the Spanish flag was made out, and it was thought that the gun boats had come out to fight, but the vessels were found to be carrying a Red Cross flag; they were hove to and boarded, when it was found that they had no papers, and that there was nearly 400 Spanish soldiers on board; they were declared prizes, the Stars and Stripes hoisted, and a prize crew put aboard the steamer Humberto Rodriquez; the Badger left the blockade and proceeded with its convoy of prizes toward Havana, which was reached on the morning of the 29th; after reporting to the flagship the Badger was ordered to take her prizes to Dry Tortugas; arriving there at noon of the 30th the Badger and her prizes lay at Dry Tortugas awaiting the action of Navy Department until August 3; painting ship and coaling the Rodriquez when orders came to deliver the soldiers in the two sailing ships to General Blanco at Havana, then send the Rodriquez to New York as a prize, and for the Badger to proceed to Key West for orders; arrived at Key West at 4 p. m.

Aug. 4. The Badger is ordered to Guantanamo, but has to coal and provision ship first, which occupied three days.

7. Started for Guantanamo, stopping at Jibara on the way; arrived there at 10 a. m. of the 9th, and found 26 American men of war and auxiliaries at anchor; the flowers of the American navy, Sampson, Schley and Watson on their flagships, New York, Brooklyn and Oregon. Badger is attached to Watson's squadron for the invasion of Spain.

10 to 12. Badger's crew are coaling ship again, and are going ashore in sections, going over the battlefields of Guantanamo, rambling all over Camp McCalla, and occasionally getting inside the Spanish lines. At 10 p. m. on the 12th, general signal to the fleet was made. Four battleships, New York and Brooklyn ordered to Tompkinsville; peace protocol signed and hostilities ceased; blockade of Cuba and Porto Rico raised, which caused intense enthusiasm all through the fleet.

13. Commodore Watson transferred his flag from the Oregon to the Badger. Peace! No more standing by your guns through the lonely night watches; peering through the darkness for the enemy and blockade runners; a little relaxation now, and probably home soon.

14. New York, Brooklyn, Iowa, Indiana, Massachusetts and Oregon leave for home with their bands playing "Home, Sweet Home," and "Out of the Wilderness." Badger's crew are enjoying themselves ashore, rambling all over the country.

16. Commodore Watson transferred his flag to the Newark.

17. Officers of the Badger go to Santiago on the Scorpion, and visit the destroyed Spanish fleet.

18. Seven officers and 182 men of the 34th Michigan Vol. came aboard the Badger, and at 4 p. m. the Badger picks up her anchor and starts for home, arriving at Montauk Point on the 23d, and arriving at Boston on the 27th. Just before getting into Boston, Coxwain Nellinger fell from the main mast head to the deck, dying very soon after; this is the only fatality of the entire cruise. The Badger lay in Boston until September 27th, much to the disgust of the Naval Reserves, who desired to get back to their occupations after the war was over. Whilst laying in Boston she participated in the naval demonstration on September 15th, '98, and put on 600 tons of coal.

Sept. 27. The Boston went to League Island Navy Yard, Philadelphia, and proceeded to take out her ammunition and stores, and dismounted her secondary battery, ready for being discharged.

Oct. 6. The Reserves were paid off and left Philadelphia in a special train stopping at Newark where they paraded, receiving a very enthusiastic welcome, a hearty welcome was also given them in Jersey City, where they were received by Governor Voorhees and staff, and they afterwards paraded in Hoboken, where the inhabitants had made elaborate preparations to receive them, and gave the boys a most vigorous reception; they then marched aboard the U. S. S. Portsmouth, where they were mustered out of the service, and received their discharges.

Oct. 10. The City of Hoboken gave the Badger crew a banquet and reception at the Quartette Club Hall, in Hoboken.

Officers of U. S. S. Badger.

Commander A. S. Snow, U. S. N., Commanding.
Lieutenant H. C. Gearing, U. S. N., Executive Officer.
Lieutenant E. McC. Peters, Navigator.
Lieutenant (J. G.) Washington Irving, Watch and Division Officer.
Lieutenant (J. G.) Irving Blount, Watch Officer.
Ensign Thomas Goldingay, Watch Officer.
Ensign Chas. M. Vreeland, Watch Officer.
Ensign Wm. P. O. Rourke, Junior Watch Officer.
Ensign Daniel A. Dugan, Junior Watch Officer.
Ensign A. N. Kemble, Junior Watch Officer.
Ensign F. Upshur, Junior Watch Officer.
Ensign C. F. Long, Marines Officer.

P. A. Engineer G. F. Burd, U. S. N., Chief Engineer.
P. A. Engineer B. F. Hart, First Assistant Engineer.
P. A. Engineer D. Ritchie, Assistant Engineer.
Assistant Engineer James Quilty, Assistant Engineer.
Assistant Engineer H. Anderson, Assistant Engineer.

P. A. Paymaster A. H. Colby.
P. A. Surgeon M. S. Simpson.
Pay Clerk Thomas Criss.

One Ensign and five men of the Battalion of the East, N. R. N. J., were detailed for the Resolute at the commencement of the war, and served on her until October 21, 1898. The Resolute was engaged in carrying troops to Cuba until early in July, when she took a cargo of submarine mines to Admiral Sampson. During the engagement with Cervera's fleet at Santiago she acted as a Despatch boat and carried the news to Sampson that the fleet was coming out of Santiago. Later she was present during the bombardment of Manzanillos.

After peace was declared she became the flag ship of Admiral Sampson and took the Peace Commissioners to Havana.

Ensign—Geo. H. Mather. Seamen—H. H. Garrabrants, C. M. Rivers, A. A. Delaney, C. Nevins, G. Schoonmaker.

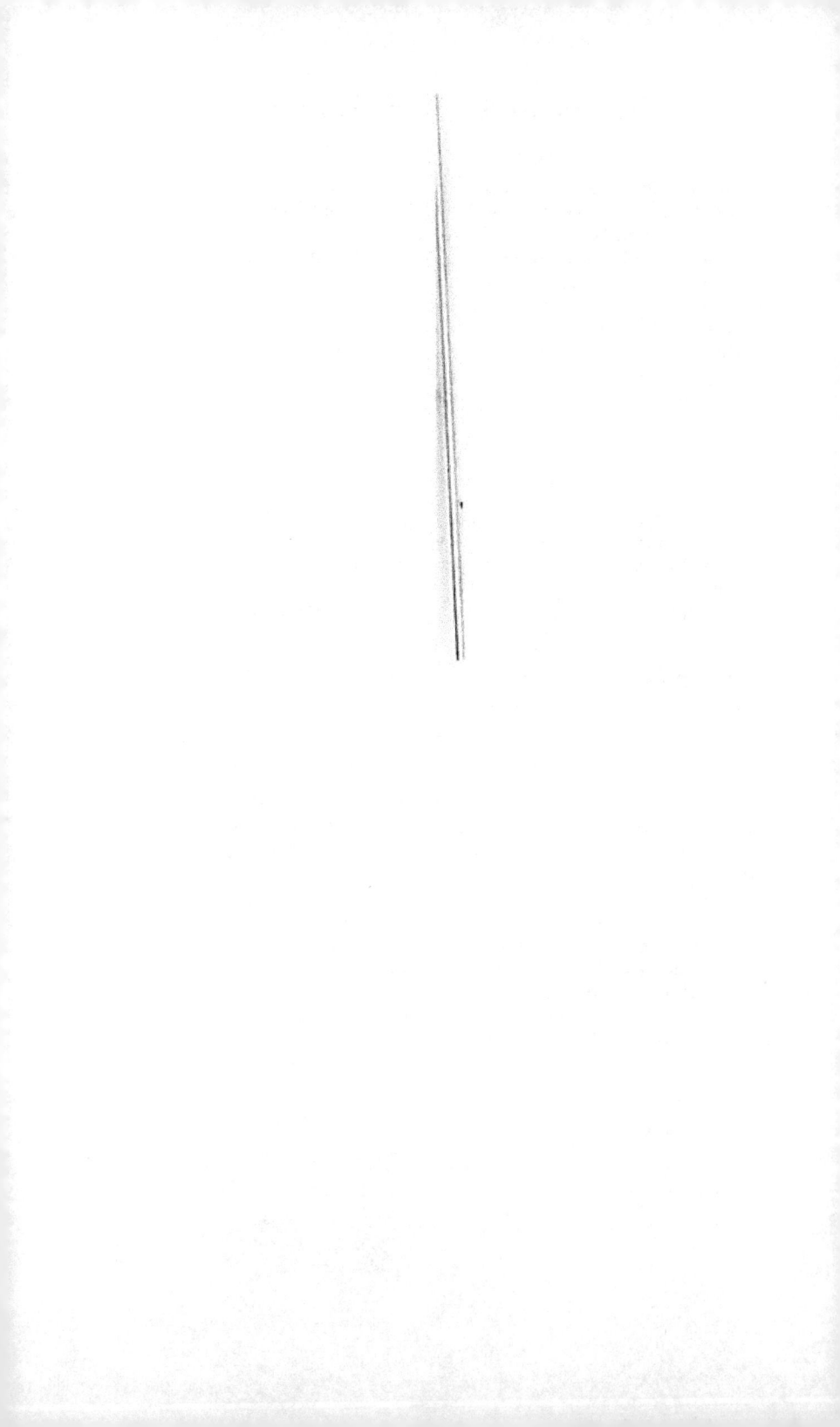

First Regiment, New Jersey Volunteers.

April 8. If the First Regiment are called upon for active service, it will assemble in fatigue uniform with overcoat, slouch hat and leggins. Canvas belts for cartridges will probably replace present cartridge box and leather belts, knapsacks or merriam packs. Each guardsman is expected to wear a good suit of underclothing, socks and flannel overshirt and stout shoes.

8. Attendance of spectators at battalion drills of the First Regiment has been so large that men have been detailed to keep crowd back.

12. Gov. Voorhees signed following commission: John C. Schock, First Lieutenant Co. M, First Regiment.

19. Companies C, D and F of the First Regiment had successful practice march to Hilton last night. At Irvington fireworks were set off in honor of the guardsmen, and many residences were illuminated.

27. Crowds gathered at the armory last night to discuss the situation and to hear latest information as to movements of the First Regiment.

27. Members of the First Regiment made individual preparations to start for Sea Girt on hearing that they had been called to represent the State in the war with Spain.

27. The First Regiment will consist of 980 enlisted men and 46 commissioned officers. The maximum strength of the companies will be 81 men and 3 officers. [United States Government standard, a company consists of 103 men and 3 officers.]

28. Members of the First Regiment get ready to move promptly on receiving orders. They select their tent mates and arrange other details.

28. The field and staff, non-commissioned staff and line officers of the First Regiment is as follows: Field and Staff, Edward A. Campbell, Col.; R. Heber Breintnall, Lieut.-Col.; Henry W. Freeman, Chas. B. Champlin, Frank Hayes, Majors; James L. Marsh, Adjutant; Andrew B. Byram, Horace K. Vincent, Arthur H. MacKie, Battalion Adjutants; Geo. W. Church, Quartermaster; Thomas H. Jones, Paymaster; Henry Allers, Surgeon; James R. English and S. Harbourne Baldwin, Assistant Surgeons; Rev. John Kellar, Chaplain; John L. Johnson, Judge Advocate; William H. Howard, Inspector Rifle Practice; Robert M. Phillips, Commandant Gun Detachment. Non-Commissioned Staff—William E. Terhune, Sergeant Major; Chas. W. Mayow, Geo. E. Melcher, Geo. H. Pennington, Battalion Sergeant Majors; Albert H. Baldwin, Quartermaster Sergeant; Geo. W. Hill, Drum Major; Rudolph E. Wilhelm, Job A. Wolverton, Wm. Pitt Rich, Hospital Stewards; Benjamin S. Sager, bugler. Co. A, Joseph H. McMahon, Captain; Patrick J. Griffin, First Lieutenant; Thomas J. Mulgrave, Second Lieutenant. Co. B, Geo. Handley, Captain; Herbert C. Van Houten, First Lieutenant; Wm. H. Camfield, Second Lieutenant. Co. C, Harry T. Spain, Captain; Alvah M. Jacobus, First Lieutenant; Wm. H. Black, Second Lieutenant. Co. D, Alfred Williams, Captain; Orrin E. Runyon, First Lieutenant; James E. Van Houten, Second Lieutenant. Co. E, James Walsh, Captain; Geo. Zimmer, First

Lieutenant; Gustavus A. Shourt, Second Lieutenant. Co. F, John D. Fraser, Captain; First Lieutenant, vacant; Sidney W. Allen, Second Lieutenant. Co. G, Geo. M. Buttle, Captain; F. Randolph Crowell, First Lieutenant; James E. Brown, Second Lieutenant. Co. H, Frank E. Boyd, Captain; Adolph G. Frey, First Lieutenant; Wm. H. Ring, Second Lieutenant. Co. I, Arthur Rowland, Captain; Frank L. Van Deman, First Lieutenant; Arthur Tomalin, Second Lieutenant. Co. K, Cornelius A. Reilly, Captain; C. Albert Gasser, First Lieutenant; Joseph B. O'Rourke, Second Lieutenant. Co. L, Theodore C. Reiser, Captain; Louis J. O'Rourke, First Lieutenant; Edward Phillips, Second Lieutenant. Co. M, Captain, vacant; John C. Schoch, First Lieutenant; Patrick J. Anderson, Second Lieutenant.

29. The First Regiment was ordered to Sea Girt. It will number over 1,000 men when they leave Newark. They will wear the uniform of the New Jersey National Guard, which will be exchanged later for the United States Government uniform. The men must be at Camp Voorhees not later than 2 p. m., Monday. With the exception of the Merriam packs, or knapsacks, they are all ready to go.

30. The First Regiment will leave the armory on Orange street at 9:30 a. m. on Monday, and march down Broad street to C. R. R. station and from thence take train for Sea Girt.

May 2. The First Regiment off for Sea Girt; a magnificent demonstration marks the departure of the Newark troops. Vast crowds watch the march of the soldiers, who so promptly responded to the call of duty. Broad street was completely blocked by a surging mass of humanity, and at the Central R. R. station the throng was so dense that it was only by hard and desperate work that the police forced a passage way for the soldiers. Many women fainted; children were tossed about, and strong men found themselves helpless in the crush. At the armory the men reported to their companies and each received his equipment, which consisted of a Merriam pack or knapsack, a haversack, a rubber poncho, an overcoat, a cartridge belt, and a tin cup. At 9:20 a. m. Col. E. A. Campbell gave the order to fall in. The drum corps took up a position in the main corridor, and at the word of command, sounded the Adjutant's call to assemble. The comamnd was given to move, and the men were under way. The mounted police went ahead to clear the way. Following the mounted police came Phil. Sheridan Post. G. A. R., headed by a drum corps. Lincoln Post Followed, led by Commander Wm. M. Whiting. In order came Garfield Post and Marcus L. Ward Post; next came two companies of the Catholic Protectory cadets of Arlington. They have been the pride of Capt. Joseph H. McMahon of Co. A, who drilled them. Hexamer Post and a company of firemen under Battalion Chief Sloan. The order of the troops was as follows: Col., Edward A. Campbell; Captain and Adjutant, R. M. Philips; Major and Surgeon, Henry Allers; Captain and Quartermaster, Geo. W. Church; Lieut. and Asst. Surgeon, James R. English; Lieut. and Asst. Surgeon, S. H. Baldwin; Captain and Chaplain, J. Madison Hare; Voss' First Regiment Band; Major Henry W. Freeman, commanding First Battalion: Captain Geo. Handley, commanding Co. B; Capt. Harry T. Spain, commanding Co. C; Lieutenant Orrin E. Runyon, commanding Co. D; Capt. John D. Fraser, commanding Co. F; Major Chas. B. Champlin, commanding Third Battalion; Capt. James Walsh, commanding Co. E; Capt. C. A. Reilly, command-

ing Co. K; Company K with colors; Capt. Joseph H. McMahon, commanding Co. A; Capt. Geo. M. Buttle, commanding Co. G; Mayor Frank Hayes, commanding Second Battalion; Capt. Theo. C. Reiser, commanding Co. L; Capt. Arthur Rowland, commanding Co. I; First Lieutenant John C. Schoch, commanding Co, M; Capt. Frank E. Boyd, commanding Co. H. The scene along Broad street cannot be described. At Market street and thence to the City Hall the crowd was the most dense. Mayor Seymour, with head uncovered, stood in the centre of the City Hall steps holding aloft an American and Cuban flag. Every available foot of standing room on the steps and balcony was occupied by city officials and others. Passing the Hall, the guardsmen marched to Hill street and countermarched to the Central depot, where trains were in waiting. Taken all in all, it was such a demonstration as the Newark soldiers will remember all their lives. It was 11:20 a. m. when the first train started for Sea Girt. Flags, hats and handkerchiefs were waiving everywhere; whistles of factories tooted, and church bells were rung, and amid all the noise the first section started. It was ten minutes later when the second section started, and there was a repetition of the wild scenes and sounds that attended the first train. The first section carrying the First Regiment of Newark, arrived at Camp Voorhees, Sea Girt, at 1:15 p. m.; there were 600 men on the train of 13 cars, including Col. Campbell and staff, the First Bat, Cos. B, C, D and F, and Cos. A, E and K of the Third Battalion. The second section arrived at 1:28. On the train was Co. G, Third Bat., under command Major Champlin, and Cos. H, I, L and M, of Second Bat., Major Hayes. The flag on Governor's headquarters was raised at noon. On the east, near the ocean, is the section assigned to the First Regiment, of Newark.

3. Gov. Voorhees was pleased with the fine showing of the men of the First Regiment. The Commissary Department slow in furnishing food, but it is nourishing, substantial and there is plenty of it. First guard mount of the camp was given by men of the First Regiment. Strict discipline is maintained, and leaves of absence few.

3. The camp at Sea Girt, as begun yesterday, sheltered 3,000, the whole number being divided as follows: First Regiment, 1,015; Second Regiment, 1,045; Third Regiment, 940; Gen. Plume's staff and a few others. Gen. Plumes' staff is composed of following officers: Col. Marvin Dodd, of Newark; Col. Alexander C. Oliphant, of Trenton; Col. Geo. W. Terriberry, of Paterson; Lieutenant-Col. William Strange, of Paterson; Lieut.-Col William S. Righter, of Newark; Col. A. Judson Clark, of Newark; Maj. James W. Howard, of Newark; Maj. Chas. Alling Gifford, of Newark, and Maj. J. S. Henry Clark, of Newark.

4. The examination of troops has begun at Sea Girt. United States medical officers reject only two members of Co. B, First Regiment. Men jubilant over success. Capt. Henry Allers, the first Jerseyman to be mustered into Government service. Private Hartman, when told that he was too old to serve, broke down and cried over his misfortune. Officers have an easier examination than the men. Rigid discipline is maintained in the camp, and few men allowed to leave the grounds. Outside guards are to be posted when the Government takes control of the post.

6. Co. B, First Regiment, was the first to be mustered into the Government service from New Jersey. Five companies of the First Regiment have been examined. A much better showing is being

made than was expected. Cos. B, C, D, F and K have gone through the ordeal; only 16 men have been rejected, three in B, three in D, five in C, four in F, and one in K.

7. The seven members of the First Regiment, who yesterday refused to enlist, were hooted out of camp at noon to-day. When their refusal became known the feeling became so bitter against them that they were kept in the guard house all night for protection. Only the bayonets of the detail prevented an assault on the unpopular guardsmen. Physical examinations are progressing rapidly and with satisfactory results. Recruits arrive to fill up the depleted ranks.

8. There was a great deal of satisfaction expressed in Co. E, First Regiment, when Gov. Voorhees, on Maj. Freeman's recommendation, had Private Herbert G. Mayhew detailed as his orderly. Private Mayhew has been in the National Guard for 10 years, and served 5 years in the regular army. The examining surgeons are hard at work all day in mess halls, so that by night every company in the First Regiment will have stood the physical ordeal. The rejections are very few, the highest being 6 men in Co. K. The work of mustering in the examined and fully recruited companies is progressing steadily, and the entire battalion was mustered in by 4 p. m.

8. Sixty-four new men for the First Regiment go down to Sea Girt to fill vacancies in the ranks.

10. Newark regiment hopes to move first. Officers and men confident that they will be assigned to the station at Chickamauga. Col. Campbell and his subordinates pass the physical examination.

12. The War Department wanted the First Regiment to move from Sea Girt to the South to-day, but Gov. Voorhees objected, as their supplies have not yet been received; not believed to be safe to have them move to the front until they are fully prepared with the necessary clothing. They will be prepared to leave by Saturday, and the military authorities hope that the three regiments will go as a unit.

13. The First Regiment receives orders to be ready in 24 hours to move. Col. Campbell and his staff sworn into the service of the United States Government. The rejection of a homeopathic physician as surgeon, causes indignation in the Second Regiment, and Gov. Voorhees may insist on the doctor's being accepted.

16. New orders for the First Regiment. Col. Campbell directed by Secretary Alger to take his command to Falls Church, Va. Must be ready for instant moving, just as soon as supplies are received the Newark soldiers will start for the South, probably by next Thursday.

18. The First Regiment men showed their joy over moving orders, by parading and doing a war dance. The First Regiment made a fine showing at its last inspection at Sea Girt.

20. Newark troops at National Capitol. First Regiment soldiers cheered on their way to their station in the South. Will leave for Falls Church, Va., this afternoon. Inspiring scene before the start from Sea Girt. Gov. Voorhees with bared head reviews the First Regiment as it leaves the camp at Sea Girt.

21. First Regiment soldiers spent the night in the woods at Dunn Loring, Va., then they moved to their station at Camp Alger. Fine weather makes the boys happy, and all of them are well.

22. Newark's soldier boys now have their tents up, and camp regularly organized at Camp Alger, near Falls Church, Va.

23. The First Regiment wants to move further South, where they will see actual service. There is some sickness and one death among the men of the First, but all are contented and well. A

new water supply has been secured, and the food is satisfactory.

24. The First Regiment men more closely guarded at Camp Alger than are the other soldiers. Their first dress parade was held yesterday at 5:30, and Col. Campbell is well pleased with the showing of the men.

25. Col. Edward A. Campbell, of the First New Jersey, has been assigned to the command of the First Brigade, First Division, at Camp Alger. The brigade is composed of First New Jersey, Seventh Ohio, and Sixty-fifth, New York Infantry. The Newark soldiers are pleased over the honor conferred upon their commander, Maj. Allers was made Brigade Surgeon. Jerseymen miss the delicacies with which they were regaled at Sea Girt, and are still disposed to grumble over army fare.

26. First Brigade drill at Camp Alger. Col. Campbell puts his new command through the evolutions in a satisfactory manner. Only two cases of slight illness in New Jersey Regiment. Twenty thousand men will be in Camp Alger by Saturday.

29. The sunshine was warmly welcomed at Camp Alger this morning.

29. A grand review was given today at Camp Alger. Yesterday was the first time in over thirty years that an army of volunteers rendezvoused in time of war, had passed in review before the commander in chief of the army and navy, and attracted many thousands from Washington. There were were 12,000 troops in line. Col. Campbell of the First Regiment, as Acting Brigadier General, led theparade, and his regiment was close behind his staff.

30. The first death in the ranks of the First New Jersey Regiment, occurred yesterday, when Corporal Wm. Chase Canniff, of Co. D, expired at the hospital after an illness of about 18 hours. His death was ascribed to acute Bright's disease. The troops at Camp Alger were given a holiday, to celebrate Memorial Day. Jerseymen feasted on chickens, and fed a hungry Kansas regiment which arrived in the grounds without equipments or provisions.

31. The First Regiment men received a welcome bundle from the Daughters of the Revolution, containing socks, pencils, postal cards, magazines, papers and pipes. The contents were distributed by the captains of the companies. A terrific rainstorm struck the camp Sunday night, and as a result every member of the First Regiment who had not thoroughly trenched around his tent, was drenched. In some of the tents the water was nearly knee deep.

June 4. The severity of army discipline was exemplified this morning, when Corporal Byrne of the First Regiment was refused a furlough to attend his mother's funeral.

7. Lieutenants Van Deman, Gasser and Van Houten ordered to Newark to secure recruits for the First Regiment at Camp Alger. First Regiment spent a long and tedious day moving camp, yesterday, to the grounds formerly occupied by the Fourth Missouri, about a mile from the First's old grounds. The camp of the First was left in splendid shape, but that was not the case in camp which they marched into. A more disreputable and dirty camp could not have been imagined than that which they entered. Before a stake was driven, every inch of the ground was swept, and the refuse burned. The new grounds are more healthy than the old.

8. Too hot to drill at Camp Alger. Battalion evolutions abandoned, because soldiers in heavy uniforms are affected by the weather. The Pennsylvania State troops tried to force the Newark boys' guard line; both sides charged bayonets, but Col. Campbell and Maj. Freeman arrived in time to prevent blood

shed. The men are worrying because of the failure of their pay to arrive.

9. The first brigade parade since the First New Jersey moved camp, was held last night. The parade ground is very rough, and is covered with the stumps of small saplings, which made marching difficult, but the New Jersey troops made a good showing. Adjutant Graff returned to duty with the regiment after serving on brigade staff of Col. Campbell. The men have a plentiful supply of water. The Seventh Ohio made a solemn compact with the First New Jersey to stand together against the Pennsylvania yaps.

11. Requisitions for ammunition lead the First New Jersey troops to believe that will be ordered to move. A detail of 8 men and a corporal were put to work constructing a bathing pond near the camps of the First New Jersey and Seventh Ohio. Suspicious characters invade the camp after the men receive their money, and are driven out after a lively chase at night. A large amount of cash was sent to Newark. A commission was appointed to investigate the division hospital.

12. Portraits—Mr. and Mrs. Roderick B. Stevens, of this city, have six sons enlisted in the First Regiment N. J. Volunteers.

13. The officers of the First Regiment were measured for clothing suitable for wear in the South, today. The new uniforms will be made of Kahki material, such as is used by English army officers in-India and Egypt.

13. First Regiment attended a memorial service conducted by Father Tom Sherman, for a dead Missouri private.

14. Heat and dust make camp life miserable, and the soldiers suffer in spite of a shower. Major Allers is at the head of a commission to investigate all the serious cases of illness in the hospitals.

New Jersey officers were entertained at a lawn fete.

14. The recruits for the First are being whipped into shape at Sea Girt.

15. A box containing housewiv bandages, tobacco and shoe strings, has been received by the First Regiment from the Needlework Guild and Nova Caesarea Chapter of the Daughters of the Revolution of Newark.

16. The First Regiment made a fine showing in the parade this morning at Camp Alger. Maj. Freeman iposed of nine cases of dereliction of duty among Jersey soltion of duty among Jersey soldiers. The First was called out to fight forest fire, which threatened the camp. The commissioners are warned that they must see that the men secure supplies of good food.

20. The First Brigade, consisting of the First New Jersey, Seventh Ohio and Sixty-Fifth New York, started this morning on a two days' practice march to Potomac River. Two days' cooked rations were issued to each man. Newark soldiers lead the way.

27. Gen. Butler praised Col. Campbell and his men, on the fine showing made while on the march. Modern guns have arrived for the First New Jersey, and the troops soon expect to have a sham battle with blank cartridges.

28. The First N. J. Regiment, while at drill yesterday, was surprised and attacked by troop A, of the N. Y. Cavalry. There was a hot skirmish as the troopers dashed among the infantrymen, but the Jerseymen rallied by squads and repulsed the cavalry. The weather was hot and the men were greatly fatigued by the unexpected assault.

July 2. The arrival in Camp Alger, last night, of the recruits for the First N. J. Regiment, resulted in a long continued ovation as the men passed down the line of regiment, before being assigned to their respective companies. There was

little sleeping in camp last night. The artesian well for the Newark ers is in working order, and the men rejoice over an abundant supply of pure water. Dr. Allers retired as Division Surgeon, and returns to his brigade at his own request.

5. Camp Alger soldiers are very enthusiastic over Sampson's victory.
6. The First Regiment's march to the Potomac River was made through rain and mud, but only one man was forced to drop out, and he was a new recruit.
7. The Newark soldiers are still held in camp. Instead of being sent to the front; two battalions are being ordered to do provost duty. They are lacking in equipments. Ninety per cent. of their old Springfield rifles have been condemned by the acting Inspector General.
9. Only one case of typhoid fever has developed in the First Regiment at Camp Alger.
10. The First Regiment at Falls Church has their reading tent.
11. The Newark soldiers have just received their pay for June.
13. Private Jeremiah Murphy, of the First N. J. Volunteers, died of typhoid fever at Camp Alger.
14. Private Murphy was buried this afternoon. The services were held at his late residence. The coffin was covered with an American flag, and with an escort of four soldiers was taken to the cemetery of the Holy Sepulchre.
15. Camp Alger soldiers wild with delight. Newark men lead the celebration in honor of the surrender of Santiago de Cuba.
21. Gen. Plume and Col. Clark visit Dunn Loring to lay out a new camp for the First Brigade.
23. Major Champlain praises fine showing of the First Regiment N. J. Volunteers at Camp Alger, Va.
26. First Regiment N. J. Volunteers visited by President McKinley and wife.
29. First Regiment N. J. Volunteers are tired of camp; they ask to go to the front.

Aug. 1. First Regiment U. S. Volunteers ordered to camp at Dunn Loring.
2. After many disappointments the First Regiment moved camp to Dunn Loring, to-day.
3. The First Regiment has been ordered to join Gen. Wade's provisional division.
4. New rifles were given the First Regiment yesterday.
6. First Regiment ordered to Porto Rico.
6. Camp Alger, Dunn Loring, was visited by a terrific rain storm; the hospital and reading room tent were blown down.
8. The paymaster arrived in camp of First Regiment.
9. It is alleged that the death of Walter J. Spawn, of Co. M, First Regiment, is due to neglect.
11. Another heavy rain storm visited Camp Alger to-day.
12. Camp Alger is doomed. The original place of that name will soon be but a memory.
19. Wm. S. Smith, of Co. C, First Regiment, died at Fort Myer hospital, yesterday morning, of typhoid fever. The members of Co. E have taken charge of the funeral arrangements, and will see that the remains are sent home.
19. Maj. Freeman of the First Regiment asked for his release from service.
20. The vote for home was put to the First Regiment; and two-thirds of the men voted for home.
21. The fifth death in the camp of the First Regiment occurred to-day. Private Thos. J. Ryan, succumbs to typhoid fever.
21. Capt. Rowland, Lieut. Philips and Lieutenant Ring resign.
21. The non-coms. gave a banquet to the non-coms. of the Seventh Ohio.
23. First Regiment once more in review before Gen. Gobin, the commander of Camp Alger, and made a fine showing, and several of the boys were overcome with the heat.

30. The Newark regiment show proud exhibition of robust vitality, only 54 men out of 1,300 are on the sick list, and only 24 in hospital, with a death roll of five. The dead are Wm. C. Canniff, Corp. Co. D, died May 29th, of acute Bright's disease; Jeremiah Murphy, Co. A, died July 13th, at Fort Myer hospital of typhoid fever and pneumonia; Walter J. Spawn, private Co. M, died Aug. 8th, at Fort Myer hospital of typhoid fever and pneumonia; Wm. E. Snith, private Co. E, died Aug. 8, Fort Myer hospital, typhoid fever; Thos. J. Ryan, private Co. G, died Aug. 21st, Fort Myer hospital, typhoid fever.
30. The boys vote once more. Votes taken by Gen. Meany and Col. Oliphant, military aides to Gov. Voorhees. Result of vote, unknown.

Sept. 1. Delay is dangerous. The boys of the First Regiment may soon reach the limit of endurance. Disease lurks near them. They are in good health now, but if kept in Virginia much longer they will soon be in the condition of the Sixty-Fifth Regiment.
2. Newark boys break camp and will start for Sea Girt this afternoon. Boys wild with delight.
3. First Regiment N. J. Volunteers arrived at Sea Girt. All the men hale and hearty, excepting 16 sick.
3. Six sick soldiers from Sea Girt arrived in Newark.
4. About 1,100 members of the First Regiment came home on furlough.
8. Gen. Plume, commander of the First Brigade is home on furlough with the boys.
12. 850 members of the First Regiment, who have been in Newark on furlough, returned to Sea Girt, and the air bit nippingly when the boys arrived.
13. 300 men from First Regiment arrived in Newark for one week's furlough.
14. The paymaster arrives at Sea Girt.

15. Back in old form; Newark boys make a fine showing in parade at Sea Girt. They march like veterans.
17. Men of the First Regiment on furlough in Newark were paid off at the Central R. R. station.
20. Officers of the First Regiment wish to join the Fourth Regiment.
20. Members of First Regiment N. J. Volunteers assembled at C. R. R. station and return to camp at Sea Girt.
24. A reviewing stand is being erected opposite the City Hall for city officials to review therefrom the First Regiment N. J. Volunteers on their arrival home from the camp at Sea Girt.
26. After five months absence the First Regiment N. J. Volunteers arrived home and were royally welcomed. The public and other buildings were decorated with flags, bunting and other devices, and the streets through which they marched were thronged with spectators.
26. Twenty-five Newarkers, recruits from the First Regiment, have returned to camp at Sea Girt, to join Fourth Regiment.
26. The First Regiment is at last home from the war. They were received by admiring thousands of citizens; the First section containing the sick men and the horses arrived in the Mulberry St. yard of the Central R. R. 12:15 p. m. to-day, the next section arrived at 1:28 p. m. Its arrival was made known by a gun fired from the roof of the Daily Advertiser. At 1:15 the gun signalled that the parade had begun. The regiment marched past the City Hall at 2:30. As the parade passed up Broad street, cheer after cheer arose from the thousands who had gathered. The sidewalks from Lincoln Park to Orange street were jammed from curbline to buildings. The windows of every building were filled and on many of the roofs the crowds had gathered. All along the line of march business houses

and private dwellings were decorated with the national colors. At the City Hall the parade was reviewed by Mayor Seymour, Monsignor Doane and Rev. Dwight Galloupe, the general committee and their friends, who were on a reviewing stand built for the occasion. The police arrangements for handling the crowds were made in advance. Each side of Broad street, from Hill street to the canal bridge, was wired off at the curb line, and no one was allowed outside of the wire. Bronzed, and with a more soldierly bearing than when they marched away, the soldiers marched up Broad street in perfect formation and with the pride of duty done written on every face. As the procession passed the Daily Advertiser, Mr. Allen, the correspondent of the Daily in all the camps of the First Regiment, was cheered to the echo. The day was one that will long be remembered by the members of the First Regiment N. J. Volunteers.

Oct. 5. Members of the First N. J. Volunteers will act as escorts for Naval Reserves on their arrival home.

HARRISON, KEARNY, ARLINGTON AND THE BOROUGH OF EAST NEWARK IN THE SPANISH-AMERICAN WAR.

In making up the account of the services rendered by the citizen soldiers and sailors who enlisted from this section of New Jersey, it is doubtful if in any other part of our country a greater number (the population considered) entered the different arms of the service, and the varied organizations in the civil, military and naval branches of the government as the facts will show, responded to their country's call for help than did the citizens of the four above named places in Hudson county, New Jersey. Almost the entire membership of the command of Capt. George M. Buttle, Co. G, First Regiment N. J. Volunteers, of 106 men, were recruited in these towns and boroughs. Of the whole number who enlisted there were 164 men, 58 of whom enlisted as follows: One joined the Astor battery, and is now serving with that organization in the Philippine Islands; another one enlisted in Roosevelt's regiment of Rough Riders, and others enlisted in the Sixth Regular Cavalry, the 22d, the 71st, the 9th and the 69th N. Y. Volunteers, and the 2d and 4th N. J. Volunteers. Of those who entered the naval branch of the service we are only able to name Assistant Engineer Lewis, a resident of Kearny, who served on the auxiliary cruiser St. Paul. One of the sorely pressed band of United States marines that landed from the U. S. S. Marblehead, near San Juan, near the city of Santiago, that withstood the repeated attacks of the Spaniards for many days, and the withering tropical July sun, was from Kearny, and he still lives to tell what he and his comrades endured. Of the 230 members comprising the crew of the U. S. S. Badger, some are from Kearny. Other hardy and spirited ones from this northern section of New Jersey will be found among the crews of the U. S. S. Yankee, and the U. S. battleship Iowa. The only person from this section (the four places her in named) and in the naval service when the late war began, was Thomas Butler. He was one of the victims of the U. S. battleship Maine, blown up in Havana harbor, February 15th, 1898. Butler was a veteran of the Civil War. Those who died from natural causes in the service of their country were as follows: Private Thomas Smith, Jno. Young, and T. J. O'Brien. The remains of all were brought to their respective homes for burial, and were interred, and where they will sleep until the reveille of the last morn shall awaken them from their slumber to appear in that grand review before the Great Commander above. For the promptness and alacrity with which the 164 stalwart sons, brothers and fathers came forward to meet the call of the government in the time of need, the citizens of Harrison, Kearny, Arlington and the Borough of East Newark were not unmindful of this practical demonstration of patriotism; for as soon as it was known that the soldiers and sailors had been allowed to return to their homes on furlough, a goodly number of the citizens of these places came together and appointed of their

number twenty-five persons and intrusted to them the duty of preparing a "Welcome Home Reception" for the soldiers and sailors who had enlisted in the Spanish-American war, and who, but a few months ago, were either their associates or neighbors. This reception took as part of the entertainment the form of a supper. The citizen's committee met the soldiers and sailors at Arlington Park, at Depot Square. The soldiers and sailors were under the command of the United States drill master connected with the Catholic Protectory, of Kearny. The Catholic Protectory Band provided the music. Headed by the band the citizens escorted the soldiers and sailors to Freeman's Hall, Arlington, (October 13th, 1898), where 254 persons sat down to a delicately prepared, but substantial meal, prepared in Davis' (of Newark) best style. The meal over the other parts of the festivities were begun by Capt. George M. Buttle, of Co. G, First N. J. Volunteers, presenting an appropriate gold medal to George W. Pearsall, First Sergeant of Co. G, as a reward to the Sergeant for his services in carrying out his (Capt. Buttle's) orders in relation to Co. G, while in the field. The other and the closing part of the gathering was the presentation by the honorary members of Co. G, (all of the members are residents of Kearny), and to them as a committee, had fallen the lot of raising the ways and means to assist the needy families of soldiers and sailors, while from their homes in the service of the government, with a beautiful silk company flag, embroidered in gold, bearing the name of "Co. G, First Regiment N. J. Volunteers." This emblem of liberty as a gift from the citizens of Harrison, Kearny, Arlington and the Borough of East Newark, was but a fitting reward on such occasion to a worthy military organization. Capt. Buttle received the flag on the part of the Company and expressed their appreciation in appropriate and eloquent remarks. With hearty cheers and the parting hand shaking, it was made manifest that "Grim-Visaged War. had Smoothed its Wrinkled Front," and that the soldiers and sailors of Harrison, Kearny, Arlington and the Borough of East Newark were about to "Hang up their bruised arms for monuments."

The officers of the Committee of Entertainment were

JOSEPH PARKER, JR., Chairman,
EDWARD A. STRONG, Secretary,
JAMES M. LOWDEN, Treasurer.

CHRONOLOGY OF THE
Spanish=American War in 1898.

January 25.—U. S. battleship Maine, Captain C. D. Sigsbee, U. S. N., is ordered to Havana, Cuba.

February 8.—The publication of a letter written by Senor Dupuy de Lome, Spanish Minister to the United States, speaking disparagingly of President McKinley, leads to the Minister's resignation of his post and the appointment of Senor Luis Polo y Bernabe.

February 15.—The U. S. battleship Maine, lying in the harbor of Havana, is destroyed and sunk by an explosion between 9 and 10 o'clock p. m. Two hundred and sixty-six lives were lost.

February 17.—Rear Admiral Sicard, commanding the North Atlantic Squadron, orders a court of inquiry into the loss of the Maine.

February 19.—The request of the Spanish officials in Havana for a joint investigation into the loss of the Maine is declined.

February 21. The United States Senate orders an investigation into the Maine disaster.

March 8, 9.—Congress votes to place $50,000,000 at the unqualified disposal of President McKinley as an emergency fund.

March 16.—Spain remonstrates against the presence of the United States fleet at Key West and against other measures of defense by our Government.

March 17.—Facts concerning Cuba stated in the Senate by Senator Proctor, of Vermont, as the result of personal observation.

March 28.—Court of Inquiry's report on the Maine sent to Congress.

April 5.—Consul General Lee recalled.

April 10.—Consul General Lee leaves Cuba.

April 11.—President McKinley sends a message to Congress recommending armed intervention in Cuba.

April 15.—Army ordered to mobilize.

April 16.—Senate belligerency resolutions passed.

April 18.—Congress votes against Cuban recognition.

April 19.—Congress passes resolutions demanding the withdrawal of Spain from Cuba.

April 20.—Queen opens Cortes with war speech. Government announces its opposition to privateering. President signs notification to the nations of intention to blockade.

April 21.—Our Minister at Madrid, General Stewart L. Woodford, informed by the Spanish Minister of Foreign Affairs that diplomatic relations between Spain and the United States are terminated.

April 21.—President McKinley cables our ultimatum to Spain, demanding a reply by April 23.

April 23.—Senor Polo y Bernabe, Spanish Minister, receives his passport and leaves Washington.

April 22.—Cuban ports blockaded by the American squadron.

April 23.—The President issues his proclamation calling for 125,000 volunteers.

April 24 (Sunday).—A Spanish decree declaring war against the United States was gazetted at Madrid.

April 25.—Congress passes a resolution declaring that the state of war existed from April 21.

April 26.—Recruiting volunteers began in New York city.

April 27.—United States vessels bombard Matanzas.

April 27.—Seventh Regiment declines to enlist.

April 28.—Commodore Dewey's fleet sails from Hong Kong for Manila.

April 29.—U. S. cruiser Yale (Paris) arrives in New York.

April 29.—Spanish squadron sails from Cape Verd for the West Indies.

April 29.—New York shells Cabanas forts.

April 30.—Commodore Dewey's squadron arrives off Manila.

April 30.—Flagship New York fires on Spanish cavalry sharpshooters off Havana.
May 1.—U. S. cruiser Topeka arrives at New York from Falmouth.
May 1.—Commodore Dewey's squadron destroys the Spanish fleet at Manila.
May 2.—Cable from Manila to Hong Kong cut by Commodore Dewey.
May 4.—Battleship Oregon and gunboat Marietta sail from Rio Janeiro.
May 7.—Commodore Dewey informs State Department of the seizure of Cavite.
May 9.—Congress thanks Rear Admiral Dewey. Governor Black disbands the Thirteenth regiment.
May 10.—The Gussie expedition sailed from Tampa.
May 11.—Ensign Worth Bagley and four of the crew of the torpedo boat Winslow killed by a shell from the Spanish forts at Cardenas.
May 12.—Admiral Sampson's squadron bombards the forts at San Juan, Porto Rico.
May 12.—The Spanish Cape Verd fleet arrives at Fort de France, Martinque.
May 12.—Gussie expedition repulsed.
May 13.—Commodore Schley's fleet sails south to meet the Spanish squadron.
May 14.—Spanish Cape Verd fleet sighted off Curacao.
May 15.—Rear Admiral Dewey reports on fall of Manila.
May 15.—Sagasta's Cabinet resigns.
May 15.—Spanish torpedo boat destroyer Terror disabled at Fort de France, Martinique.
May 15.—Spanish fleet leaves Curacao.
May 15.—General Merritt ordered to the Philippines as Military Governor.
May 15.—Governor Black authorizes reorganization of disbanded 13th regiment.
May 17.—Sagasta's new Cabinet announced at Madrid.
May 18.—Ninety thousand troops ordered to mobolize in Chickamauga.
May 22.—Spanish fleet arrives at Santiago de Cuba.
May 22.—Cruiser Charleston sails for Manila.
May 23.—Troops A and C arrived at Camp Alger, Falls Church, Va.
May 24.—The Spanish fleet is bottled up at Santiago.
May 25.—Three transports with 2,588 men start for Manila.

May 25.—President issues a call for 75,000 more volunteers.
May 26.—Oregon arrives in Key West.
May 26.—One of Spain's Cabinet Ministers said the country was willing to accept "an honorable peace."
May 26.—Commodore Schley is in touch with the insurgent leaders.
May 26.—Ninth and Sixty-ninth regiments of New York arrive at Chattanooga.
May 26.—Florida expedition landed without opposition near Guantanamo, Cuba.
May 27.—Spanish scout ships chased by American warships near Key West.
May 29.—Commodore Schley reports the trapping of Cervera in the harbor of Santiago de Cuba.
May 29.—Cruiser Columbia arrives at New York, having been in collision with the British steamship Foscolia, which sank.
May 30.—Troops embark at Tampa for Havana.
May 31.—Rear Admiral Sampson's fleet bombards forts of Santiago de Cuba.
June 1.—Transports for Manila arrive at Honolulu, H. I., and the Boys in Blue become the guests of the city.
June 1.—Monitor Monadnock ordered to Manila from San Francisco.
June 2.—Spain again appeals to the Powers to intervene.
June 3.—American squadron bombarded Santiago de Cuba.
June 4.—Lieutenant Hobson sinks cruiser Merrimac in the mouth of the harbor of Santiago de Cuba.
June 6.—Cable communication between Santiago and Hayti ceased at midnight.
June 6.—Fortifications of Santiago de Cuba reduced.
June 7.—American squadron bombards and silences batteries at Santiago.
June 7.—Monitor Monterey and Collier Brutus sail for Manila.
June 8.—Assault on fortifications of Guantanamo Bay.
June 9.—House agrees on war revenue conference report.
June 10.—Admiral Sampson reports he has held Guantanamo Harbor since the 7th.
June 10.—Senate agrees on conference report on war revenue bill.

June 10.—Marines from the Panther land at Caimanera.
June 11.—Four Americans at Caimanera are killed in a fight with the Spaniards.
June 13.—32 transports with Shafter's troops sail for Santiago.
June 13.—President McKinley signs the War Tax bill.
June 14.—Two Americans and several hundred Spaniards killed in a battle at Caimanera.
June 15.—Second expedition sailed from San Francisco for Manila.
June 15.—Great destruction results to the Santiago forts through the use of the dynamite guns on the Vesuvius.
June 17.—Spanish squadron sailed from Cadiz and passed Gibraltar.
June 20.—Transports with General Shafter's troops arrive off Santiago.
June 22.—Part of Shafter's troops landed.
June 23.—Balance of troops landed without accident.
June 23.—Admiral Camara's Cadiz fleet arrives at Island of Pantellaria.
June 24.—Sixteen American soldiers killed and forty wounded in driving back Spanish soldiers at Santiago.
June 27.—Commodore Watson to command fleet to attack Spanish home territory.
June 27.—President McKinley recommends thanks of Congress for Lieutenant Hobson, and that he be transferred to the line.
June 28.—President proclaims blockade of Southern Cuba from Cape Frances to Cape Cruz.
June 29.—General Shafter reports he can take Santiago in 48 hours.
June 29.—The Senate thanks Lieutenant Hobson and his men, naming each one personally.
June 30.—Egyptian Government refused to let Camara coal his fleet at Port Said.
July 1.—Shafter's army began the assault upon Santiago de Cuba, capturing the enemy's outer works.
July 2.—Shafter renewed the attack upon Santiago, losing about 1,000 in killed and wounded, and making 2,000 Spanish prisoners. The Spanish casualties probably exceeded those of the Americans.
July 3.—Cervera's fleet destroyed at Santiago, with great loss of life.

July 6.—Spanish transport Alfonso XII. blown up off Mariel by American gunboats.
July 6.—Hobson, the hero of the Merrimac, and his comrades exchanged for Spanish prisoners outside Santiago.
July 7.—President signs Hawaiian annexation resolution.
July 7.—Admiral Dewey took Subig and 1,300 prisoners.
July 11.—Cruiser St. Louis brings Admiral Cervera and 746 prisoners to Portsmouth, N. H.
July 11.—Admiral Sampson's fleet bombarded Santiago.
July 13.—Announced that yellow fever has broken out in General Shafter's army.
July 14.—General Toral and the Spanish army surrendered Santiago at 3 p. m.
July 17.—"Old Glory" raised over Santiago at noon.
July 18.—President issues a proclamation providing for the government of Santiago.
July 18.—Seven American vessels bombard Manzanillo and destroy seven Spanish ships.
July 21.—General Miles, with 3,415 men on transports, convoyed by warships, starts to take Porto Rico.
July 21.—American gunboats captured Nipe and sank the Spanish cruiser Jorge Juan.
July 21. British steamer Newfoundland captured by Mayflower, while trying to run blockade at Havana.
21. Gen. Miles starts for Porto Rico with his troops, conveyed by strong fleet.
21. Garcia resigns and his troops withdrawn to mountains.
21. Dewey authorized to attack Manila.
21. Gen. Leonard R. Wood made Military Governor of Santiago.
21. In an attack on Manila rebels repulsed with great loss.
22. Gen. Shafter instructed to consult with Gen. Garcia.
22. Gen. Garcia instructs his troops to return to their former occupations.
22. Cabinet decides to conciliate Cubans.
22. Sampson opened port of "Nipe" as a base.

22. War Department orders 20,000 men to Porto Rico.
22. Camara's squadron headed toward Centa.
22. Cuban Junta repudiates Gen. Garcia's course.
22. Second expedition to the Philippines disembarked near Manila.
22. Rio Janeiro sails for Manila with 900 men.
23. Porto Rico expedition leaves Tampa, Fla.
23. Miles' troops pass by Hayti.
23. Spanish Admiral Camara's fleet at Cartagena, Spain.
23. American flag raised at Nipe.
23. Gunboat Mangrove captured Spanish sloop Aguldita, off Cuba.
23. Hospital ship Relief brings 125 wounded soldiers from battlefields of Cuba to New York harbor.
24. Spanish Admiral Cervera says our navy is magnificent, and he feels no disgrace in having been beaten by such a foe.
24. U. S. S. Frolic sailed for Key West and will join blockading squadron off Cuba.
24. Gen. Brooke and staff left for Newport News this afternoon.
24. Camp Alger troopers ordered to move to Porto Rico.
24. Tampa troopships carrying 4,000 men sail for Porto Rico.
24. Lieut Hobson makes arrangements for saving Spanish battleships, Cristobal Colon and the Infanta Maria Teresa.
24. Gen. Shafter reports deaths among soldiers from yellow fever.
24. Major James E. Stewart has been appointed postmaster at Santiago.
July 25. Gen. Shafter issued order praising army for bravery at Santiago, Cuba.
25. Rear Admiral Dewey believes Philippine rebels can govern themselves better than Cubans.
25. Spanish Admiral Camara will use Centa as his base of operations.
25. Troops A & C, N. Y. Cavalry, and Third Illinois Infantry, reached Newport News to take transports for Porto Rico.
25. Sampson's report in President's hands.
25. Shafter's army to have rest; entire Fifth Corps will be ordered north.
25. Cubans protest against Gen. Shafter's treatment of Gen. Garcia.
25. Dissensions in Red Cross Society in Cuba; Dr. Gintera has resigned and returned to the U. S.
25. Post office in Santiago, Cuba, begins business.
25. Gen. Shafter reports more surrenders.
26. Gen. Miles begins landing troops near Ponce, Porto Rico.
26. Mrs. J. Addison Porter at Santiago, Cuba, reports that at battles of El Caney and San Juan, sharpshooters shot wounded soldiers on Red Cross litters.
26. Transport Hudson arrived at Fort Munroe with wounded officers from Santiago, Cuba; bodies of Hamilton Fish, Jr., and Captain Capron were brought back on same transport.
26. Submarine mines exploded off Willetts Point, N. Y.
26. Engraved thanks of Congress forwarded to Admiral Dewey at Manila.
26. Insurgents capture Gibara, Cuba.
26. Hospital ship Relief, released from quarantine.
26. 5,000 men of Gen. Brooke's command arrived at Newport News to embark for Porto Rico.
26. Uncle Sam bought tug, Gypsum King.
26. Porto Rican army of invasion will use 2,000 whistles to enable scouts to keep track of one another.
26. Russian war ships sail from Manila.
26. Spanish prisoners from outlying garrisons are pouring into Santiago, Cuba.
26. Surgeon Gen. Sternberg came to New York to investigate condition of sick and wounded on Seneca.
26. Gen. Shafter's Fifth Corps to go to Montauk Point.
26. Sampson's fleet to be divided.

26. Gen. Shafter is feeding 11,000 Spanish prisoners.
26. Gen. Shafter publicly praises his men; no army ever equaled it, he says.
26. Transport Morgan sailed for Porto Rico with troops.
26. Steamer Olivette sailed with hospital stores and nurses for Santiago, Cuba.
27. Spain asks our peace terms.
27. Surgeon Gen. Sternberg criticises Red Cross nurses.
27. Gen. Grant left Chickamauga Park for Newport News, Va., to embark for Porto Rico.
27. Merritt-Chapman Wrecking Co. off for Santiago, Cuba.
27. Admiral Sampson gives praise to all engaged in fight at Santiago.
27. Review at Camp Alger.
27. Our flag planted on Porto Rico at Guancio by sailors from gunboat Gloucester.
27. Gen. Shafter reports dead and wounded.
27. Hercules Powder Co. at Pinole blown up; five men killed and thirteen wounded.
28. Gen. Shafter cabled War Department that customs are being collected at Santiago.
28. Gen. Shafter reports 3,770 of his troops sick.
28. The news that Hawaii had been annexed to U. S. reached Honolulu by steamer Coptic, on July 13th.
28. Surgeon Gen. Sternberg reports that accounts of conditions of Seneca on her trip from Santiago with sick and wounded soldiers has been exaggerated.
28. 3,770 soldiers sick at Santiago, Cuba.
28. Spaniards fall back on San Juan, Porto Rico.
28. P. J. Besosa, a native Porto Rican, is acting as scout and interpreter for Gen. Miles.
28. Transport Massachusetts takes Gen. Brook expedition to Porto Rico to reinforce Gen. Miles.
28. Tampa, Florida, abandoned as military base.

28. Report of Capt. Chadwick, of New York, Capt. Taylor, of Indiana, Capt. Philip, of the Texas, and Lieut. Commander Wainwright, of the Gloucester. Each officer praises bravery and gunnery of their respective crews.
28. Typhoid fever spreading at Camp Alger.
29. President McKinley preparing to resist possible obstruction of European powers in peace negotiations.
29. Brig.-Gen. F. C. Harris sailed from Newport News for Porto Rico.
29. Transport Concho reached Hampton Roads with 176 ill and wounded officers and men from Siboney, Cuba.
29. Sagasta sends notice of peace overture to Spain's Cabinet Council.
29. Secretary Alger orders Gen. Shafter to move his army in Santiago, Cuba, to Montauk, L. I.
30. Gen. Miles received surrender of Ponce, Porto Rico, without firing a shot.
30. Gen. Miles captured Yanco, Porto Rico, the terminal of railroad leading to Ponce, Porto Rico.
30. In fight preceding capture of Guanica, Porto Rico two captains and two privates of Sixth Massachusetts Volunteers were wounded.
30. Gen. Miles makes Gen. Wilson Military Governor of Ponce, Porto Rico.
30. Auxiliary cruiser St. Paul left Newport News with the First Ohio Regiment to join Gen. Brooke's expedition to Porto Rico.
30. Reserve fleet of Spain is being assembled at Cadiz, Spain.
30. President McKinley placed reply to Spain's plea for peace in Ambassador Cambon's hands.
31. Admiral Dewey reports that insurgent leader Aguinaldo has assumed bold attitude of defiance.
31. French steamship, Maneaubia, captured off Porto Rico by gunboat Dixie.

31. U. S. transport Rio Grande arrived in N. Y. harbor.
31. Capt. Charles Dodge, of Twenty-fourth U. S. Infantry died of yellow fever at Santiago, Cuba.
31. Hospital ship Solace left Brooklyn Navy Yard for Cuba to distribute medical supplies.

Aug. 1. Residents of San Juan, Porto Rico, flee from the city on approach of the U. S. troops, under Gen. Miles.
1. Gen. Miles reports his victories and that he has collected $14,000 in duties.
1. Gov.-Gen. Augusti, of Manila, calls on Spain for help to resist American attacks.
1. Battleship Texas arrives in N. Y. harbor from Santiago to be docked and cleaned.
1. Spanish soldiers retreating toward San Juan, Porto Rico, are pillaging towns and maltreating women.
1. Transport Concho and Alamo arrived in New York from Santiago with sick and wounded soldiers.
1. Government transport, Michigan, sailed for Santiago, Cuba, with provisions for the army.
1. All of the 150 passengers from Santiago, Cuba, brought by Saratoga are in Detention Hospital at Egmont Key.
1. Transport Concho reported worse than the Seneca. She has 191 sick passengers; five died on the way from Siboney, Cuba.
1. Third Pennsylvania U. S. Volunteers ordered to Ferdinandina, Fla.
1. Gen. Henry's division consisting of 3,400 men and 26 pieces of artillery, has been ordered from Yanco to Ponce.
2. Mayor of Yanco, Porto Rico, issued proclamation expressing joy for taking of city by U. S. troops.
2. Astor battery landed in Philippines.
2. Gen. Linares' appeal to Madrid for permission to surrender made public.

2. Gunboat Eagle captured Spanish schooner, Dolores, loaded with provisions for Batabano, Cuba.
3. Gen. Garcia in heavy fight at Mayari, Cuba.
3. Surgeon General advises removal of troops from Camp Alger on account of fever.
4. Spain's reply to President McKinley leaves no room for doubt that she will accept peace terms.
4. Eighteen regiments from as many States (20,000 men) will be sent to Porto Rico, under Gen. Wade's command.
4. Gun boat Bancroft captured Spanish sloop off the Isle of Pines.
4. Between 30,000 and 50,000 American troops will be assigned to Cuba for garrison duty.
4. Battleship Texas safely placed in dry dock No. 2 at Brooklyn Navy Yard.
4. Cruisers St. Louis and St. Paul ordered north to be disarmed.
5. Gen. Shafter reports 3,788 soldiers ill at Santiago, Cuba.
6. Captain Gen. Macias, of Porto Rico, instructed by Spanish government to capitulate.
6. Cape Juan, about 30 miles east of city of San Juan, Porto Rico, taken by men from American warships.
6. Second Division marched from Camp Alger and are encamped at Bristow.
7. Spain's Cabinet accepted basis of our peace terms.
7. Guayama, Porto Rico, surrendered.
7. Official reports show that fleet in Cuban waters is practically free from sickness.
7. An army officer declares military balloon is a failure, and that its use at Santiago caused death of 300 men.
7. Five companies of First N. Y. Regiment, sailed from San Francisco, Cal., for Honolulu, Hawaii.
8. Rough Riders under Col. Roosevelt start from Santiago, Cuba, for home.
8. Inhabitants of Cardenas informed commander of Hudson that they would not resist attack.

8. Capt. Sigsbee has been placed in command of the battleship Texas.
8. Spain's reply to peace demands received in Washington.
8. Gen. Miles is closing in on San Juan, Porto Rico.
10. Spaniards attacked American troops at Malate, near Manila, and were driven back with heavy losses.
10. Guantanamo, Cuba, has formally surrendered, and Brig.-Gen. Ervers has been made Military Governor.
11. The Alicante and three other vessels have sailed from Guantanamo Bay with Spanish prisoners, and the St. Louis with the 9th and 10th Infantry.
12. Gen. Schwan's brigade had general engagement near Hormiguers, Porto Rico; Americans victorious.
13. Orders have been issued placing Mangrove out of commission.
13. Greater U. S. made by stroke of the pen that humbles Spain.
13. Arrival of transport Sequranca in N. Y. harbor from Santiago, with 331 men.
14. Our peace terms with Spain are: 1st, Spain to relinquish all sovereignty over the Island of Cuba; 2d, Spain to cede to U. S. the Island of Porto Rico, and all islands under sovereignty of Spain in West Indies; 3d. Spain to cede to U. S. Island of Guam in the Ladrones; 4th, U. S. to hold bay and city of Manila pending conclusion of treaty of peace; 5th, commissioners were appointed by U. S. to meet commissioners on part of Spain to conclude treaty of peace.
14. Cuban Junta orders cessation of warfares.
14. Cable censorship has been raised.
14. Transport Gate City arrived at Montauk Point from Santiago with 500 men of the Third and Sixth Cavalry.
15. Admiral Dewey captures Manila after bombardment, before receiving word from Washington in regard to treaty of peace.

16. Secretary of State, William R. Day and Senator Cushman K. Davis, of Minnesota, were appointed on the peace commission.
16. Gen. Blanco has resigned as Governor and Captain-General of Cuba.
16. Gen. Augustin has resigned as Governor-General of Philippines.
16. Italy was the first nation to send congratulations on close of war.
17. Ambassador Hay has accepted portfolio of U. S. Secretary in Cabinet.
17. Cubans at Santiago have decided to respect peace agreed to by U. S.
17. So great is the mortality in Spanish camp at Santiago that victims of disease are burned.
17. Spanish troops massacred 90 citizens of Ciales, Porto Rico.
18. The Seventy-first N. Y. Volununteers, of N. Y., now in camp at Montauk Point, L. I.
18. Monitor Nahant put out of commission.
19. Col. Theo. Roosevelt with eight troops of Rough Riders, and Gen. Joseph Wheeler with 22 troops of third regular cavalry, arrive at Camp Wikoff, Montauk Point, L. I.
19. Gen. Blanco, Gen. Castellanos, Gen. Leon and Admiral Manterola, appointed commissioners for Cuba, and Gen. Macias, Gen. Ortega and Admiral Vallaimo for Porto Rico.
19. The transports Seneca and Comanche arrive at Montauk Point, L. I., with the 24th and 25th Infantry, U. S. Regulars, from Santiago.
19. Hospital ship Relief brought 248 sick and wounded soldiers from Porto Rico to New Jersey.
20. Review of the victorious warships at New York.
20. Transport Mobile arrives at Montauk Point, L. I., with 1,600 men from Santiago.
20. Transport Olivette arrives at Newport News with 200 sick soldiers from Santiago.

21. Gen. Merritt cabled to Washington articles of capitulation of Manila.
21. Lieut. Hobson presented to Geo. F. Philips, one of the Merrimac heroes, a gold watch, on behalf of citizens of Galveston, Texas.
21. Transport Rio Grande brought 600 colored Regulars from Santiago to Montauk Point, L. I.
22. Four transports. Breakwater, Olivette, City of Macon and Mortera, arrive from Santiago.
22. President McKinley has decided to retain the island of Luzon.
22. 75,000 people were at Tompkinsville to see our warships.
22. Transport Arizona leaves San Francisco with 1,300 troops for Manila.
22. American transports Peru and Pueblo arrive at Manila with 2,000 men on board.
23. Admiral Sampson in consultation with Cuban commissioners, who will accompany him to Cuba.
24. Natives of Porto Rico make trouble for the United States on belief that liberty gives them the right to punish their former Spanish masters.
24. The sunken vessel that obstructed entrance to San Juan harbor, Porto Rico, has been removed, and ships can now pass in.
25. Gen. Garcia makes his report to the Cuban Junta.
26. The Peace Commission decided on by the President will be composed of following named gentlemen: Secretary William R. Day, of Ohio; Senator Cushman K. Davis, of Minnesota; Senator William P. Frye, of Maine; Justice Edward Douglas White, of Louisiana, and Mr. Whitelaw Reid, of New York.
26. Capt. Chas. E. Clark, of the Oregon, is at the Naval Hospital, Brooklyn.
26. Dynamite cruiser Vesuvius arrived in New York harbor.
26. Gen. Shafter sailed from Santiago.
26. Admiral Schley on duty again on the Brooklyn.
27. Commodore John W. Philip has been assigned to command North Atlantic squadron.
28. Second Regiment N. Y. Volunteers in Jersey City.
28. Private of Marines O'Shea fired the first shot at Cervera's fleet on July 3d from bridge of Oregon.
29. U. S. transport San Marcus arrived in New York harbor with 600 men from Key West.
29. Auxiliary cruiser Yankee arrived in New York harbor with the First Naval Reserve Battalion of New York. (
29. N. Y. Merchants' Association shipload of supplies distributed at Montauk.
30. Seventy-first N. Y. Volunteers arrived home in New York.
30. U. S. warship New Orleans enters San Juan harbor, Porto Rico; first American war vessel to enter port of San Juan since war began.
30. Gen. Garcia relieved of his command by Gen. Gomez.
30. 229 members Eighth Regiment N. Y. Volunteers, arrived in New York.
30. Battleship Massachusetts left New York for Boston.
30. Official report of Spanish Admiral Montejo of destruction of his fleet in Manila bay.
30. Lieutenant Hobson arrived at Santiago on steamer Sequranca, to raise Spanish cruisers, Cristobal Colon and Infanta Maria Teresa.
31. First woman to hold army officer's commission, is Assistant Surgeon Anita Newcomb McGee, U. S. A.

Sept. 1. Col. Roosevelt's Rough Riders are being mustered out.
1. Hospital ship Olivette sank in harbor of Fernandina, Fla.; no lives lost.
1. Admiral Schley and Gen. Gordon sail on the Seneca for Porto Rico as commissioners to arrange terms for evacuation of Porto Rico.

1. Admiral Cervera and his officers and men were ordered released, Spain agreeing to pay for their transportation home to Spain.
1. Admiral Schley with his staff sails for Porto Rico.
1. Gen. Miles and staff sailed on transport Obdam from Porto Rico for United States.
2. Gen. Shafter and staff arrived at Camp Wikoff, Montauk Point, L. I.
2. Spanish transport Isla DePanay from Santiago, arrived at Corunna, Spain, with detachment of surrendered Spanish troops.
2. Transport Shinnecock arrived from Montauk with 318 sick soldiers for New York city hospitals.
2. The New York, Paris, St. Louis and St. Paul returned to International Navigation Co.
2. Justice White declined place on peace commission.
2. N. Y. Naval Reserves sailed from League Island Navy Yard for New York.
3. Troops A & C, N. Y. Volunteer Cavalry sailed from Ponce, Porto Rico, for New York on transport Mississippi.
3. The first cargo of coal for Porto Rico since the war began, was shipped from Baltimore, Md., on schooner James F. Beachan.
3. All the regulars at Montauk Point ordered to posts occupied by them before the war.
3. Naval parade at Boston, Mass.
3. Filipinos still fighting; grabbing all lands possible before peace terms are signed.
3. Gen. Blanco packing up and preparing to leave Cuba.
3. Spanish transport Covadenga arrived at Santander, Spain, with 2,200 Spanish soldiers from Santiago, Cuba.
3. War Department issued order for mustering out Seventy-first N. Y. Volunteers.
3. The N. Y. Naval Reserves marched through New York streets, and were received by Mayor Van Wyck and President McKinley.
4. Spain names Senors Montero Rios, Castillo, Villanrutia and Gen. Cerero as peace commissioners.
4. 80,000 volunteers have been ordered mustered out.
4. Spanish gunboat Sandoval, scuttled in Guantanamo Bay, after Gen. Toral's surrender was floated and will be added to our navy.
5. Gunboat Gloucester, Lieut.-Commander Wainwright, arrived in New York harbor.
5. Gen. Brooke left Guayma, Porto Rico, for San Juan.
5. Lieut.-Col. Smart, a war department scientist, has gone to Camp Wikoff, Montauk Point, to investigate water supply.
5. Col. Roosevelt made farewell address to the Rough Riders.
5. Transports Roumania and Unionist arrived to-day at Camp Wikoff with 686 soldiers from Santiago.
6. Gen. Aguinaldo now holds the Manila water works; a menace to American forces.
6. Gen. Shafter assumes command of Camp Wikoff.
6. Rear Admiral Sampson, Major-Gen. Wade and Major-Gen. Butler, the Cuban military commission, sailed for Cuba on the Resolute.
6. Gen. Brooke has arrived at suburbs of San Juan.
6. Transport Alleghany wrecked off Point Judith with 113 soldiers on board; all saved.
7. Rear Admiral Schley and Gens. Gordon and Brooks arrive at San Juan, Porto Rico, and call on Spanish Gen. Macias.
7. Approximate estimate that war has cost United States $114,500,000.
7. Transport Chester arrived in New York harbor with Fourth Regiment Penn. Volunteers.
7. Owing to Gen. Blanco's refusal to receive Red Cross supplies, American troops may be sent to Havana to take place of Spanish soldiers sooner than had been planned.

7. Secretary Alger made announcement that he will make a tour of various camps.
8. Gen. Miles and the Third Wisconsin Volunteers arrived on the Obdam.
9. Spain instructs her commissioners.
9. Transport Alliance arrived at Honolulu with Third Battalion of First N. Y. Volunteers.
9. Eighth Regiment N. Y. Volunteers arrived in New York.
9. Gen. Miles reached Washington.
9. Gen. Shafter left Washington with orders to report to Adjt.-Gen. Corbin.
9. Admiral Cervera goes to Boston and Portsmouth to see about shipping his sailors home.
10. Troop C, N. Y. Volunteers, of Brooklyn, arrived on Transport Mississippi.
10. Twenty-first N. Y. Volunteer Infantry moves from Camp Black to Camp Meade, its first step toward Cuba.
10. Spanish war prisoners from Annapolis arrive in New York and go on City of Rome to Portsmouth, N. H.
10. Surgeon-Gen. Sternberg ordered all patients in Camp Wikoff to be sent to city hospitals.
10. Territory of Hawaii is name Annexation Commissioners will recommend to Congress.
11. Hospital ship Missouri landed 248 sick soldiers at Camp Wikoff from Santiago.
11. Gen. Blanco receives Cuban peace commissioners from United States.
12. Spanish Minister of Marine, Senor Annon, admits that he advised Admiral Cevera to make dash out of Santiago, rather than blow up ships.
12. Gen. Miles issued peremptory orders for all troops to leave Camp Wikoff.
12. War with America has cost Spain $400,000,000, besides loss of colonies and ships destroyed.

12. Spanish instructions have been received and Porto Rican commissioners will begin work today.
13. Admiral Cervera, his staff and 1,700 Spanish prisoners sailed on City of Rome for Santander, Spain.
13. Rear Admiral Dewey considers situation in Philippines as critical.
13. Rough Riders under Col. Roosevelt mustered out.
13. Lafayette Post, G. A. R., will give "Old Glory" to every school in Porto Rico.
13. A committee has been formed of Cubans to help in governing Cuba.
14. Cruiser Brooklyn ran hard aground off Guantanamo. Cuba.
14. Gen. Shafter submitted his report on Santiago campaign to War Department.
14. Aguinaldo, leader of insurgents, given two days to withdraw his troops from vicinity of Manila.
14. Col. Roosevelt and his Rough Riders part with cheers and tears.
14. Cuban Commission have taken quarters in Hotel Trotcha, Havana.
14. U. S. transport Santiago, Captain Johnson, arrived from Santiago via. Montauk, with 9,000 rifles surrendered by Spaniards.
14. Sixth Regiment Ill. Volunteers arrived in New York on transport Manitoba from Ponce, Porto Rico.
14. Three hundred officers and men and 22 nurses arrived at Montauk from Santiago on Vigilancie.
14. Military Board, consisting of Major Stanhope E. Blunt, Major Daniel M. Taylor, Capt. Beverly W. Dunn and First Lieut. Geo. W. Burr, all of Ordinance Department, appointed to investigate comparative merits of arms used by army.
14. Two Hundred and Second Regiment N. Y. Volunteers leave Camp Black for Camp Meade, Penn.
14. Spanish Cortes adopted Peace Protocol.

14. Rough Riders presented Col. Roosevelt with "Broncho Buster" in bronze, just before they were mustered out.
15. Capt.-Gen Blanco accuses United States of treachery.
15. Spanish Cruiser Cristobol Colon cannot be saved.
15. Aguinaldo leaves suburbs of Manila.
15. Spaniards destroy official records in San Juan, Porto Rico.
15. Of 225 officers and men who went to Santiago from Governor's Island, 113 returned.
15. Orders for dispersal of Eastern Squadron issued by Secretary Long, Commodore, to be commandant at Mare Island Navy Yard.
15. Battleships Oregon and Iowa ordered to Manila.
16. Maj.-Gen. Wilson and three batteries of artillery, who took part in Porto Rican campaign, arrived in New York harbor on transport Concho, from Ponce.
16. Gen. Gomez asks Spaniards to help him to get rid of Americans.
16. Final instructions have been given to the U. S. Peace Commission.
16. Capt. Evans, of the Iowa, was relieved of command at his own request. He will be placed on naval inspection board.
17. U. S. Peace Commissioners sailed on Campania for Paris, France, to meet Spanish Commissioners.
17. Gen. Toral, who surrendered Santiago, was mobbed in Vigo, Spain.
17. Aguinaldo thanks Americans and wants them to withdraw from the Philippines.
17. Spain has chosen her Peace Commissioners.
17. Manila's revenue for first month, $540,000.
17. Sampson now has 31 ships.
17. Almo arrived from Ponce, Porto Rico, with 533 officers and men of Gen. Brooke's Corps.
17. All ready for evacuation in Porto Rico; terms have been arranged by commission; Spaniards only wait for transports.
18. Peace Commissioners appointed by Spain are Senor Montero Rios, Gen. Cerebos and Senors Abarzuza, Villarrutta and Garmica.
18. San Juan defences show how well American seamen aimed.
18. Wreckers have recovered to six-inch guns from the Maria Teresa, and expect to float the ship.
18. Twenty-three per cent. of soldiers in Porto Rico are ill and General Brooke has asked for hospital ship.
19. Peace commissions are all filled; Paris commission will be: American—Judge Day, Senator Davis, Senator Frye, Senator Gray, Whitelaw Reid; Spaniards—Montero Rios, Senor Abarzuza, Senor Garmica, General Cerero, Senor Villarruta. Cuban commission: American: Admiral Sampson, Gen. Wade, Gen. Bates; Spaniards—Admiral Manterola; Gen. Parrado; Marquis of Montoro. Porto Rico commission: American—Admiral Schley. Gen. Brooke, Gen. Gordon; Spaniards — Admiral Vallarmo, Gen. Ostega, Senor Delalgulla.
19. Rough Riders parade streets of New York in their yellow uniforms, and seem to be having a happy time.
19. U. S. Commissioners agree that all Spanish troops who may desire, may remain in Porto Rico.
19. Admiral Montojo was suspended by Madrid Council of War.
19. Eight Spanish soldiers with yellow fever compose all that is left of Toral's army at Santiago.
19. Spanish Archbishop Nazaleda wants United States to annex Philippines.
20. One lesson learned from the war is necessity for high speed in war vessels.
20. Spain wants until Feb. 28th, 1899, to evacuate Cuba: not satisfactory to United States.
20. American occupation of Cuba has begun. The Stars and Stripes wave over Hotel Trotcha, Havana.

20. About 12,000 regulars will be stationed in Cuba; 1,000 in Honolulu; 3,000 in Philippines, and 4,000 in Porto Rico for garrison duty.
20. Unsuccessful attempt was made to poison Aguinaldo at Manila.
21. Secretary Alger, Quartermaster-Gen. Ludington and Surgeon Gen. Sternberg, were accused face to face by Gen. Sanger, Brig.-Gen. Wiley and other officers as being responsible for camp horrors at Chickamauga.
21. The transport Mississippi from Camp Wikoff brought the horses of Roosevelt's Rough Riders, consigned to Col. Amos S. Kimball. Dept. Quar.-Gen., to be sold at auction. The animals were brought ashore at E. 24th St. at 2 a. m. This hour was selected because many of the horses are unmanageable by ordinary men, and yielded only spirited obedience to most expert broncho busters. All more tractable horses were taken off first, leaving about 50 wild ones to the last. They got along very well until they reached 2d Ave. just as an elevated train came along, when they gave a snort and flew up the street and did not stop until corraled at 130th St. They were finally stowed away in the barns of the auctioneers. The average price received for the horses was $30. Perry Tiffany was there trying to find horse ridden by his brother, Lieut. Tiffany, and secured the animal for $45. Many of the Rough Riders bought their old mounts. At close of sale it was announced that 400 bronchos had netted about $12,600.
21. We now control two-thirds of the island of Porto Rico.
21. Spaniards grant American commissioners' request that duties be waived on Red Cross Relief supplies.
21. American commissioners instructed to take possession of public lands in Porto Rico, as safeguard.
21. Aguinaldo, leader of the Filipinos, has smuggled Maxim guns and Mauser rifles into Malolos.
22. The transports Seguranca and Mexico arrived in New York harbor with sick soldiers from Santiago and Siboney.
22. Admiral Cervera and his men arrive at Santander, Spain; crowds cheer for Cervera.
23. Two commissioners sent by Aguinaldo arrive at San Francisco, Cal.
23. Admiral Dewey used $47,000 worth of ammunition at Manila.
23. Admirals Sampson and Schley used about $100,000 of ammunition at Santiago, Cuba.
23. Government lost nearly $34,000 on horses bought for Roosevelt's Rough Riders.
23. Capt. Gen. Blanco has pardoned 119 persons exiled for all kinds of crimes.
23. Admiral Dewey wants the Philippines; he would read the riot act to any nation claiming a foot of them.
24. War Inquiry Board now complete, is composed of the following: Gen. Greenville M. Dodge, of New York; ex-Gov. A. N. Woodbury, of Vermont; Col. James A. Sexton, of Chicago; Capt. Evan P. Howell, Atlanta; Charles Denby, Indiana; Gen. John M. Wilson, chief of engineers; Thomas Livermore, Massachusetts; Gen. Alex. McDowell McCook, New York.
24. Spaniards peremptorily notified that they must not delay in leaving Cuba.
24. United States Peace Commissioners arrived at Queenstown.
24. Gen. Stewart L. Woodford resigned as Minister to Spain.
24. Gen. Garcia returned to Santiago and was honorably welcomed.
25. United States Peace Commissioners arrived in Liverpool, and were received by United States Consul James Boyle.
25. Rev. Dr. H. K. Carroll, of New Jersey, appointed commissioner for Porto Rico to examine and report on customs and requirements of our new possession.

25. Miss Jessie Schley, peace advocate, will petition President McKinley to deal generously with Spain.
25. Admiral Cervera says that Spain lived in dreams.
25. Eight Colonels and Lieutenant-Colonels were made Brigadier-Generals of volunteers, for service at Santiago, and one for services in Porto Rico.
25. Gen. Dodge was elected chairman of War Inquiry Commission.
25. Aguinaldo, chief of Philippine insurgents, says that they trust Americans to save them from Spanish misrule, and that all allegations of treachery toward Americans are unfounded and unjust.
26. Lieut. Hobson has successfully raised the Spanish cruiser, Infanta Maria Teresa, and is now on her way to Guantanamo Bay.
26. Admiral Dewey captured rebel steamer with 7,000 rifles on board at Manila.
26. War Inquiry Commissioners will begin work by looking into the Ordnance Department.
27. American Peace Commissioners and two of the Spanish Commissioners arrived at Paris, France.
27. War Inquiry Board met in secret session.
27. Lieut. Hobson having raised the Teresa, now proposes to raise the Colon and come on her to New York.
27. United States cruiser Buffalo has been ordered to join Admiral Dewey at Manila.
28. The American Peace Commissioners held their first session to systematize the working force.
28. War Inquiry Board will investigate the whole war plans of campaign, Summer camps in Florida, transports held after embarkation of troops, sons of somebodies, etc., and has asked Secretary Alger and his subordinates for specific answers to many questions.
28. The battleships Oregon and Iowa have received hurry orders to proceed to Manila.

RELIEF COMMITTEES.

May 19. The Board of Trade takes steps to create a fund in the interests of the wives and children of soldiers in cases where the bread-winner has gone to fight for Uncle Sam.
22. The Women's First Auxiliary of Newark, for the relief of soldiers' and sailors' families, has been *formed to give relief to the dependent ones left behind.*
June 1. The *Board of Trade* Relief Committee is doing a noble work. Many families of volunteers are being relieved from day to day. Members of the committee prepare 10,000 circulars in which the work is outlined and the necessity for additional contributions explained.
4. The Women's *First Auxiliary* of Newark, for the relief of soldiers and sailors, held a meeting today and received encouraging reports from the committees. The chairman, Mrs. William S. Lambert, reported that six families had been provided for.
4. The *First Roseville Relief Association* held a meeting yesterday and discussed ways and means to aid families of Roseville soldiers. They are preparing a list of entertainments, to raise funds.
4. The *Red Cross* Relief Committee of *Orange* raised $9.00 during the last week.
15. Miss Clara Barton and Mrs. John Addison Porter have gone to Tampa to do Red Cross work.
July 7. The women of the Auxiliary Committee of the Board of Trade distributed 152 checks, amounting to about $1,000 yesterday.
10. At the meeting of the Letter Carriers' Association Tuesday night it was decided to send reading matter to the soldiers at the front.
Aug. 25. Roseville Relief Association makes report to Secretary James M. Reilly of Board of Trade, of Newark, N. J.
Sept. 11. Liberty Relief Auxiliary will give entertainment to swell relief fund.
16. Members of Relief Committee of Board of Trade of Newark, will do all in their power to obtain employment for returning soldiers and sailors, and to assist their needy relatives.
20. Board of Trade Relief Committee turned over to the Women's Auxiliary Committee 170 checks, aggregating $440.

FIELD AND STAFF OFFICERS.

EDWARD A. CAMPBELL............................Colonel
R. HEBER BRIENTNALL................Lieutenant-Colonel.
*HENRY W. FREEMAN...............................Major
CHARLES B. CHAMPLIN..............................Major
FRANK HAYES....................................Major
ALVIN H. GRAFF.....................Regimental Adjutant
ANDREW B. BRYAM..1st Lieutenant and Battalion Adjt.
ARTHUR H. MAC KIE.1st Lieutenant and Battalion Adjt.
*ROBERT M. PHILLIPS......................First Lieutenant
GEORGE W. CHURCH..........Captain and Quartermaster
HENRY ALLERS......................Major and Surgeon
JAMES R. ENGLISH....1st Lieut. and Bat. Asst. Surgeon
S. HARBOURNE BALDWIN.1st Lieut. and Bat. Asst. Sgn.
HORACE W. PATTERSON...1st Lieut. and Bat. Asst. Sgn
J. MADISON HARE................Captain and Chaplain

* Resigned.

NON-COMMISSIONED STAFF.

GEORGE E. MELCHER..................Sergeant Major
GEORGE H. PENNINGTON.....Battalion Sergeant Major
JOHN HUMMELL............. Battalion Sergeant Major
JOHN COSTELLO...............Battalion Sergeant Major
LOUIS PHILIBERT.....................Chief Musician
THOMAS J. HILL....................Principal Musician
WILLIAM H. BOEH ....Principal Musician
W. PITT RICH.....................Hospital Steward
RUDOLPH E. WILHELM..............Hospital Steward
JOB A. WOLVERTON.................Hospital Steward

COMPANY A.

OFFICERS.
JOSEPH H. M'MAHON....Captain.
PATRICK J. GRIFFIN..1st Lieut.
THOMAS J. MULGRAVE.2d Lieut.
WILLIAM M'DERMOTT.1st Sergt.
MICH'L F. O'BRIEN..Q. M. Sergt.
EDWARD BRADY........Sergeant.
EDWARD J. WALSH....Sergeant.
MICHAEL LEONARD...Sergeant.
THOMAS B. O'BRIEN. Sergeant.
JAMES ROSSITER.... Corporal.
JOHN LUMON.. ....Corporal.
BERNARD MULLIN....Corporal.
JOHN WALSH............Corporal.
SIMON COX.............Corporal.
JOHN O'MARA..........Corporal.
MICHAEL O'HARE......Corporal.
PATRICK CREAN.......Corporal.
JOHN RYAN............Corporal.
WALTER WALSH........Corporal.
LUKE M'TAGUE.........Corporal.
JOHN MONAGHAN.......Corporal.
PETER M'LAUGHLIN...Artificer.

JOHN EARLY............Wagoner.
WILLIAM LEE............Musician.

PRIVATES.
THOMAS ANDERSON.
ANDREW AGNEW.
THOMAS BALLENTINE.
CHARLES BRADLEY.
HUGH BOLES.
WILLIAM BOYLAN.
JOHN J. BOYLE.
EDWARD BOYLE.
JAMES BRADY
JAMES BECKOM.
JOSEPH CRAWLEY.
THOMAS COSTELLO.
MICHAEL CARLAN.
JOSEPH CORBETT.
JAMES CULLEN.
STEPHEN CURREN.
JOHN CONWAY.
JAMES DOLAN.
MATTHEW DOUGHTY.
HENRY DENNY
JOHN DALY.
MICHAEL DWYER.
MICHAEL DUNNION.

JOHN EGAN.
RICHARD ENNIS.
MICHAEL FARLEY.
EDWARD FARRELL.
PATRICK FITZGERALD.
JAMES FAY.
THOMAS FARRAHER.
JEROME GRANT.
ANDREW GARRY
JOHN GARRITY.
JAMES GILSENAU.
JOHN GRIFFIN
JOHN GALLIGAN.
OWEN HART
THOMAS HIGGINS.
MAURICE HANNIGAN.
JOHN KENNEDY.
JOHN KENNY.
WILLIAM KEHOE.
WILLIAM KANE.
ANDREW LESLEY.
JOHN LAMONT.
THOMAS LUMON.
PETER LAFFIN.
JOSEPH LOCKART.
EDWARD LOUGHMAN.
JAMES MITCHELL.
JAMES MADDEN.
JOHN MURPHY.
JAMES MURPHY.
JAMES MAHAFFEY.
DENNIS M'CARTHY.
CHARLES M'MANUS.
ROBERT M'GARVEY.
SAMUEL M'GILL.
JOHN M'DERMOTT.
JOHN M'GLADE.
JAMES M'GEE.
JAMES M'CANN.
PETER M'ENROE.
CHARLES O'CONNOR.
JAMES O'ROURKE.
FRANK PATTERSON.
JOHN RIORDAN.
PATRICK J. RYAN.
PATRICK K. RYAN.
THOMAS REGAN.
ROBERT REILLY.
THOMAS REILLY.
THOMAS ROSSITER.
MICHAEL RODGERS.
DENNIS SLATTERY.
JAMES SHEEHAN.
JOHN G. SODEN.
PETER SCHEERER.
MILES SWEENEY.
ROBERT TUITE.
STEPHEN TIGHE.
JOHN TULLY.
EDWARD WELSH.
JAMES WHALEN.

COMPANY B.

OFFICERS.

GEORGE HANDLEY .....Captain.
H. C. VAN HOUTEN ..1st Lieut.
WM. H. CAMFIELD......2d Lieut.
WM. H. NEWMAN.....1st Sergt.
H. E. JACOBUS........Q. M. Sergt.
JOHN B. WALLACE....Sergeant.
HARRY STUART........Sergeant.
GEORGE E. WATT, JR..Sergeant.
V. A. NAPOLIELLO......Sergeant.
GEORGE S. WARD.......Corporal.

WILLIAM HARRIS.......Corporal.
HENRY RUCK...........Corporal.
MICHAEL J. HEENEY...Corporal.
PHILIP J CAHILL.......Corporal.
THEODORE KERSTING.Corporal.
JAMES M. BURNS........Corporal.
WM. B. SCHAUB, JR.....Corporal.
EDWARD FELDMAN....Corporal.
MAX MAYR..............Corporal.
WILLIAM H. KRAUSE. .Corporal.
ROBERT F. KELLETT...Corporal.
JOHN GOLDEN ....Musician.
GEORGE INGLE..........Musician.
WILLIAM H. WESTON.....Bugler.
WILLIAM E. YORKS. ...Artificer.
JOHN F. DOOLING ...Wagoner.

PRIVATES.

JOHN ARNOLD.
ROBERT BECK.
JOHN BRADLEY.
ULYSES J. BRANDIS.
JOSEPH BRUNNER.
RICHARD BURDICK.
THOMAS W. CAHILL.
FRANK M. DENNIS.
FRANK A. DONNELLY.
HENRY DONOHUE.
THEODORE C. DORAN.
JAMES P. DOWD.
PERCY L. DYER.
OWEN FARLEY.
GEORGE H. FELTZ.
PHILIPP FLEISCHMANN.
JOHN GILMORE.
JOHN GRUEBEL.
CORNELIUS V. HALL.
BERNARD A. HAMILTON.
PATRICK HAMILTON.
FRANK A. HANRAHAN.
JOHN F. HARRIS.
GEORGE HARTMAN.
JOHN HAWKEY.
WILLIAM H. HAYDON.
RUDOLPH HEILES.
HENRY W. HEYDECKE.
FRANK J. HOPKINS.
FRED J. HOWARD.
FRANK HUNTLEY.
JOHN HUSTON.
ROBERT HYLAND.
ALONZO JACKSON, JR.
ALBERT E. JENKINS.
JOHN F. KEENAN.
WILLIAM KING.
OTTO A. LEBERT.
JOSEPH LEMON.
WILLIAM R. LODER.
JOSEPH H. LONGCOR.
PHILIP S. LONGCOR.
JOHN F. LUTZ.
GEORGE H. MACDONALD.
WILLIAM MANNING.
JACOB MAUCH.
PATRICK M'CAFFREY.
DANIEL M'CAULEY.
PATRICK M'GOVEREN.
PETER J. M'HENRY.
WESLEY S. M'LORINAN.
WILLIAM F. L. MOORE.
JOSEPH MOORE.
EDWARD J. MORRIS.
FRANK A. MULROY, JR.
WILLIAM F. MURPHY.
JOHN J. MURRAY.
AUSTIN NEIRY.
EMORY A. ODELL.

JOSEPH OTT.
WILLIAM D. PANGBORN.
WILLIAM PURCELL.
J. VICTOR PURDY.
THOMAS M. QUINN.
ANDREW RAHM.
WILLIAM REA.
CHARLES H. ROBB.
WILLIAM J. SCOTT.
DOUGLAS SIMMONS.
THOMAS J. SMITH.
CHARLES SMITH.
THOMAS K. SMITH.
HENRY SMALL.
CHARLES H. SPICER.
ERNEST G. STAUBER.
EMIL STREIT.
ABRAM TURBETT.
WILLIAM VAN HOUTEN.
WILLIAM VAN WERT.
A. EDDY YARD.

COMPANY C.

OFFICERS.

HARRY F. SPAIN.........Captain.
ALVAH M. JACOBUS....1st Lieut.
WILLIAM H. BLACK....2d Lieut.
MORTIMER C. MUNN.....1st Sergt.
CHAS. P. CLINTON...Q. M. Sergt.
JOHN C. OSBORN.......Sergeant.
CARY J. M'ALLISTER...Sergeant.
GEO. O. THEURICH.....Sergeant.
PAUL J. KUNDLE.......Sergeant.
DORA C. M'ALLISTER..Corporal.
JOHN WEBER, JR......Corporal.
HARRY C. CURREY.....Corporal.
JOSEPH S. BALDWIN...Corporal.
HENRY C. KEUTZ......Corporal.
WILLIAM A. DUNN.....Corporal.
CARL H. RABKE.......Corporal.
H. E. ZIMMERAN......Corporal.
HENRY H. ROLFES.....Corporal.
JOSEPH H. DWETZ.....Corporal.
WM. J. CAMPBELL.....Corporal.
H. F. DOMBROWSKY....Corporal.
CHARLES HILTON.......Artificer.
WILLIAM H. BARTON..Wagoner.
JOS. C. HIGLESTER....Musician.
JOHN H. PRICE........Musician.
THOMAS FOX.............Bugler.

PRIVATES.

JOHN ADAMS.
JOHN ANDERSON.
HARRY E. BARTON.
JAMES BARTON.
ROBERT BARTON.
JOHN J. BROADWOOD.
OSCAR BROWN.
RICHARD M. BROWN.
FRANCIS J. CALLAN.
WILLIAM G. CAMPBELL.
JOHN J. CLUSMAN.
JOHN CULLEN.
MILLARD J. DE VAUSNEY.
EDWIN DOUGHERTY.
RICHARD J. DOWNEY.
ARTHUR S. ELLIS.
FRANK V. ERHARD.
HYMAN ETTENSON.
LE ROY S. FALES.
PATRICK FESTA.

FRANK B. GALE.
WILLIAM G. GUIGER.
FRANK M. HACKETT.
BARTLETT HAMMOND.
HERMAN E. HANK.
EDWARD HELMSTEADER.
WILLIAM HENSLER.
HERBERT V. HENDTLASS.
JOHN A. HIGGINS.
MARTIN J. HIGGINS.
OTTO HOCHADEL.
CHARLES HOLLE.
WILLIAM C. HOLLISTER.
CLAY M. HUDSON.
ABRAHAM JORALEMON.
ALBERT E. KANE.
JOSEPH KIERNAN.
ANDREW J. KLITCH.
FRED KRAEMER.
FREDERICK KULL.
ARTHUR F. LAWRENCE.
LAWRENCE LIEBERMAN.
WILLIAM M'CANCE.
THOMAS M'DERMOTT.
JAMES M'GUILEY.
WILLIAM E. M'KAY.
JOHN J. MADDEN.
OSCAR MARTIN.
ALBERT E. MEIER.
CHARLES F. METZGER.
FRANK MILLER.
FRANK MURPHY.
THOMAS ODGERS.
BERNARD J. O'ROURKE.
CHARLES PERL.
HENRY C. PETERSON.
JULIUS PIEPER.
ALFRED H. J. POOLE.
JOSEPH RAYBERT.
ARTHUR J. ROYCE.
HENRY ROPKEE.
GEORGE SAUER.
ALBERT SEIFERT.
CHARLES J. SLADE.
PHILIP J. SMITH.
EDWARD SNYDER.
CHARLES STEVENS.
HUGH L. C. STEVENS.
E. FRANK STILLWELL.
HUGH TAFT.
WALTER D. TAYLOR.
JULIUS E. THIER.
WILLIAM R. FREUSCH.
LOUIS K. VAN HOUTEN.
HENRY J. VETTER.
GEORGE F. WALSH.
JOHN A. WEBBER.
WILLIAM WICKELHAUS.
ARTHUR J. WIGMORE.
JOHN WILSON.

COMPANY D.

OFFICERS.

ORRIN E. RUNYON.......Captain.
H. C. H. STEWART......1st Lieut.
J. F. VAN HOUTEN......2d Lieut.
WILLIAM F. FLOOD....1st Sergt.
ALEX. W. BEST......Q. M. Sergt.
H. C. TOWNLEY, JR..... 2d Sergt.
F. J. RIEDINGER.........3d Sergt.
S. A. M'ILRAVEY........4th Sergt.
WILLIAM C. MILLS.....5th Sergt.
GEORGE GOETZ..........Corporal.
WILLIAM A. BROOKS...Corporal.

T. J. M'LAUGHLIN.......Corporal.
FRANK HAULE.........Corporal.
ELLWOOD A. FENTON......Corp.
THOMAS RITT............Corporal.
JOHN T. CUFF............Corporal.
HENRY A. WOLFF.......Corporal.
JAMES FALLON..........Corporal.
ALEXANDER ELLOM...Corporal.
CHARLES KREBS........Corporal.
ELMER E. SCHOOLEY..Corporal.
HENRY E. CORCORAN...Artificer.
CHARLES H. M'GUIRE..Wagoner.
H. J. TICHENOR.........Musician.
JOHN H. M'LEAR........Musician.
PETER VETTER.........Musician.
BENJ. M. WOODRUFF....Bugler.

PRIVATES.
MANNING BILBY.
WILLIAM C. BALDWIN.
JAMES BALDWIN.
ROBERT BARCLAY, JR.
WALTER H. CONNER.
EMMONS H. CRUMP.
CHARLES F. DANNEBERGER.
EDWARD J. DIXON.
WILLIAM A. DEVEY.
JOHN DAVIS.
FREDERICK W. FRANK.
ARTHUR FRITZEN.
CHARLES L. GREENFIELD.
HERBERT R. HALL.
CHARLES HETZ.
GEORGE A. HEOYS.
HARRY L. HAYTHOEM.
WILLIS E. HICKS.
GEORGE B. HONIG.
WILLIAM B. HEALD.
ROBERT L. HEALD.
CLARENCE C. HOWELL.
CHARLES P. JOHNSON
PETER H. JENSEN.
JOHN W. KIRKPATRICK.
GEORGE R. KELLY.
ANSON W. LEONARD.
GEORGE LETTS.
J. WERNER MESSMER.
FRANK MANN.
WILLIAM H. MOORE.
FRANCIS M. NESTOR.
JOHN S. OLDKNOW.
GEORGE A. PULLIS.
JACOB T. PUDNEY.
NELDEN REILEY.
TERRENCE F. REILLY.
THOMAS ROBSHAW.
WILLIAM F. SMITH.
THEODORE F. SOWERS.
SAMUEL SYKES.
OLIVER H. SPENCER.
SYDNEY H. SPENCER.
FREDERICK C. TOWNLEY.
EDWIN C. TUTTLE.
ARTHUR F. VINCENT.
JOHN T. WAER.
BENJAMIN F. WOODRUFF.
WILLIAM C. WALKER.
EDWARD R. WARNER.
FRANK H. WILT.
FRED N. ROBARGE.
WILLIAM U. ROMAINE.
JOHN STUSSY.
JOSEPH SMITH.
EDWIN F. SCHWARTZ.
FREDERICK SCHWABE.
ALBERT SCHMIDT.

FREDERICK SCHENCK, JR.
JAMES L. RIKER.
WILMER MUNCH.
FRANK M'CARROLL.
PETER M'GUIRE.
JOHN LANDELL.
HERMAN KRASOWSKIE.
WALTER J. KELLY.
WILLIAM M'INTOSH.
DANIEL F. DONOHUE.
FREDERICK BAIER.
PETER CASSIDY, JR.
PATRICK J. CONLEY.
FERDINAND LAUER.
PETER VETTER.
JAMES P. DWYER.
JAMES F. MARKEY.
THOMAS MAYLAND.
HERMAN WILLICH.
CHARLES BANSPOCK, JR.
FRANK M'FEELY.
ALBERT EVANS.
WILLIAM OELER.
MICHAEL ROSENBERG.
MICHAEL MASKELL.
ALEXANDER ELLAM.

COMPANY E.

OFFICERS.
JAMES K. WALSH........Captain.
GEORGE ZIMMER.......1st Lieut.
GUSTAV A. SHOURT....2d Lieut.
CHAS. W. BEARDSLEY..1st Sergt.
WM. C. SCHAEFER....Q. M. Sergt.
PETER J. DOPF.........Sergeant.
JOHN W. MORGAN......Sergeant.
TONY MAIER.............Sergeant.
VERNON POLK...........Sergeant.
MICHAEL P. GREEN....Corporal.
JAMES NAGEL..........Corporal.
LOUIS DOPF.............Corporal.
JOHN HELD..............Corporal.
EDWARD PIGGOTT......Corporal.
M. H. RICHARDSON....Corporal.
FREDERICK GREACEN.Corporal.
JOHN BECK........ ....Corporal.
WILLIAM J. SMITH......Corporal.
JOSEPH HUEBNER......Corporal.
WILLIAM H. AYRES.....Corporal.
F. E. KUEBLER..........Corporal.
ELMER HANDY..........Wagoner.
THOMAS BELL............Artificer.
JOHN A. MULRIHILL..Musician.
ROYAL A. GIBSON......Musician.
JOHN BEALE..............Bugler.

PRIVATES.
THOMAS ALEXANDER.
FRANK AUGERSTEIN.
JOSEPH E. ARALDO.
JOHN A. BIEN.
EUGENE BARNES.
EDWARD BASTIAN.
LOUIS BACHTOLD.
JOHN B. BRENNAN.
WILLIAM BLUMENBAUM.
JOHN DOERR.
WALTER DRAKE.
JOHN H. DORSEY.
PETER DANNEBAUM.
BENJAMIN ENTNER.
AUGUST ELBRECHT.
WILLIAM ENDERSBY.

HENRY FRANK.
JOHN F. FALLON.
WILLIAM H. FRANCISCO.
ROBERT D. FORREST.
GEORGE GREENE.
WILLIAM HENSLER.
JOHN HENNESSEY.
JOHN W. HEINDELL.
CHESTER E. HOAGLAND.
WILLIAM HILL.
THEODORE F. HAYS.
JOSEPH HEINRICH.
EDWARD F. JORAGER.
LEMUEL W. JACOBUS.
RICHARD JACOBSON.
WILLIAM JOEHNIG.
JOSEPH KILIAN.
WILLIAM C. KUEBLER.
JOHN M. KANE.
WILLIAM K. LYNASEN.
CHARLES LYNCH.
HERBERT G. MAYHEW.
JOHN F. MEEHAN.
HARRY MOSHER.
HOWARD MERRELL.
JOHN MERTZ.
JOHN M'KOSKY.
EDMUND MAYER.
HENRY W. NEALL.
JAMES J. O'DONNELL.
JAMES J. O'ROURKE.
GUS OFFER.
JOHN J. PHILLIPS.
WILLIAM PETERSON.
OTTO PETERSON.
FRANK PARK.
JAMES A. POLLARD.
CHARLES RICHARD.
JOHN REILEY.
CHARLES SPEER.
ROBERT SIMPSON.
FREDERICK STAEHLE.
WALLACE G. STEPHENS.
CHARLES STOLLBERG.
ROBERT STIRRAT.
WALTER STEITZ.
CHARLES SEIDL.
EDWARD F. SMITH.
WILBUR J. SHUPE.
JOSEPH SPIRO.
ROBERT D. SMITH.
WILLIAM TRONSON.
JAMES TERWILLIGER.
JOHN TREMBLEY.
EDWARD R. TAYLOR.
CHARLES F. TREMBLE.
WILLIAM R. THOMPSON.
LESLIE VAN HISE.
ANTON G. WEIPPERT.
HAROLD WAKEFIELD.
JAMES F. WALSH.
CHARLES WEIPPERT.
CHARLES WOLF.

COMPANY F.

OFFICERS.

JOHN D. FRASER..........Captain.
ROBERT BERRY..........1st Lieut.
SIDNEY W. ALLEN......2d Lieut.
T. J. SATCHWELL.........1st Sergt.
JAMES E. FOYLE......Q. M. Sergt.
JOHN J. LAWRENCE....Sergeant.
JAMES L. WALLACE....Sergeant.

M. J. COSTELLO..........Sergeant.
EDWARD J. VOGEL......Sergeant.
HARRY H. BEATLY......Corporal.
LOUIS HAGGERTY......Corporal.
GUSTAVE A. TATZSCH..Corporal.
WILLIAM C. KLEIN......Corporal.
LOUIS P. NIPPERT......Corporal.
BERNARD J. HAMILL...Corporal.
LOUIS W. EHLERS......Corporal.
FREDERICK HUMMEL..Corporal.
ASA P. TAYLOR..........Corporal.
SHERMAN E. WHITE....Corporal.
SAMUEL MINNIS.........Corporal.
RAYMOND KINNEY.....Corporal.
FRANCIS N. ERHARD..Artificer.
WM. S. P. EDUARDO....Wagoner.
CHARLES DOREMUS...Musician.
RICHARD L. TUCKER..Musician.
GEORGE A. DIXON......Musician.

PRIVATES.

WILLIAM ALLMAN.
ROBERT N. ARBUCKLE.
JOHN BERGEN.
JOHN T. BANKS.
STEPHEN J. BLANEY.
FREDERICK D. BELCHER.
DAVID BRYSON.
FREDERICK BROWN.
JAMES BROWN.
FRANK W. CONRAD.
HARRY R. CONRAD.
WALTER M. CONRAD.
DANIEL A. CLEARY.
JAMES CUDDY.
JOHN CASHMAN.
ALBERT B. CLAYTON.
JAMES CLIFTON.
JAMES CAUFIELD.
DANIEL F. DEVINE.
MICHAEL DURR.
FLORANCE DONAHUE.
JOSEPH E. DONNELLY.
JOHN EVERS.
FRANK ELLIOTT.
EDWARD ERHARD.
CHARLES ERHARD.
WILLIAM ERHARD.
PATRICK J. FOX.
JAMES B. FLINN.
WILLIAM R. FLINN.
JOSEPH FERGG.
JAMES A. FITZGERALD.
WILLIAM G. FRANCISCO.
WILLIAM R. GILLARD.
BERNARD GARRITY.
JOHN M. HIGGINS.
WILLIAM HAIGHT.
ELMER HARRIS.
HENRY E. HAHN.*
GEORGE A. HENRY.
JAMES HANNA.
ALBERT P. HOGLE. (Disability; discharged.)
JOSEPH HOLLAND.
CHARLES HOLLE.
THOMAS KYTE.
FRED. E. KIES.
FRED LAWRENCE.
FREDERICK C. MORGAN.
PAUL MULLER.
CORNELIUS MELVILLE.
BENJAMIN MUEHRMANN.
THOMAS MACCALLUM.
HUGH MACDONALD.
ALEXANDER E. M'DOUGALL.
ROBERT H. M'DOUGALL.

RAPHAEL M'CARTHY.
SAMUEL MORTIN.
CHARLES MORTIN.
WILLIAM J. MORROW, JR.
EDWARD A. MURPHY.
CHARLES MOELLER.
WILLIAM J. NOLTE.
FRANK A. OSBORN.
WILLIAM OBERST.
BENJAMIN PEARCE.
EDWARD L. PURCELL.
JOSEPH E. RENAUD.
WILLIAM RENAUD.
GEORGE STOUTENBURGH.
JOHN J. SHIELDS.
WILLIAM S. SLACK.
EDWARD SCHULTIES.
JOSEPH SIRISKY
PATRICK J. STRANGE.
EDWARD SCHEFFICK.
JAMES SMITH.
WILLIAM SULLIVAN.
CLARENCE E. WARD.
GEORGE WEIDELL.
FREDERICK L. WEBER.
NELSON R. WHITE.
HARRY J. WEAN.
WILLIAM WHITFIELD.

COMPANY G.

OFFICERS.

GEORGE M. BUTTLE....Captain.
F. R. CROWELL..........1st Lieut.
JAMES E. BROWN........2d Lieut.
GEO. W. PEARSALL....1st Sergt.
FRED STILES.........Q. M. Sergt.
LEONARD F. PHYLIKY.Sergeant.
WM. M. FORREST......Sergeant.
PATRICK J. CONERS...Sergeant.
CHARLES HOLLAND....Sergeant.
WILLIAM J. GRAY.......Corporal.
PRESTON LA BAW......Corporal.
JAMES A. CARROLL....Corporal.
ABRAM COTTRELL......Corporal.
WM. S. DATESMAN......Corporal.
OTTO W. FLIEDNER....Corporal.
WILLIAM GAUNT........Corporal.
C. L. EDMONDS, JR......Corporal.
WALTER A. ROBERTS..Corporal.
D. ARTHUR PAULSON..Corporal.
WILLIAM A. WHYTE....Corporal.
ERNEST BUEHLER......Corporal.
JAMES SEBALD..........Musician.
AUGUST ARNOLD.......Musician.
H. N. FRASER, JR.......Musician.
WALTER H. PIERSON..Artificer.
WM. L. ADRIANCE......Wagoner.

PRIVATES.

ALVAH W. ABEL.
GEORGE M. ADAMS.
ROBERT ALSTON.
WILLIAM G. AMANN
PETER F. BOYLE.
THOMAS BOYLE.
DENNIS BREEN.
WALTER D. BROCK.
WILLIAM J. CARROLL.
WALTER C. CHECKERSON.
ELMER CHOLLET.
WALTER J. CLARK.
RUSSELL L. CONDIT.

JOHN M. CONKLIN.
DANIEL F. COOK.
WILBUR E. CORNELL.
HOWARD W. CREED.
HARRY CREGER.
NEWTON DAVIES.
WALTER J. DEANEY.
JOHN DEENEY.
ALEXANDER J. DICKSON.
JAMES E. DOBBS.
JOSEPH H. DONOHUE.
WILLIAM A. DOUGHERTY.
ADOLPH DREUTLER.
HARRY FELMLY.
PETER S. FORREST.
GEORGE FRAZEE.
THOMAS R. FURZE.
CHARLES R. GEORGI.
AUGUST E. GROTHE.
THEODORE F. HARRISON.
JOSEPH H. HARRISON.
FREDERICK HOLZWORTH.
ROBERT HORAN.
HARRY JARVIS.
JOHN H. JONES.
WALTER C. KENANN.
OSCAR W. KOCHER.
ARTHUR B. KRATZ.
FREDERICK LAY.
ALEXANDER J. LEDDEN.
THOMAS LYTLE.
JAMES MADDEN.
GARFIELD MAJOR.
THOMAS E. MELVILLE.
HOWARD E. MONK.
OSCAR L. MOORE.
PATRICK MURRAY.
EDWARD J. MUTCH.
JOHN M'GIVNEY.
THOMAS M'GRATH.
HENRY L. NEBINGER.
ROBERT NEILL.
CHARLES F. NOLAN.
JOHN S. NORRIS.
ROBERT J. NORTON.
WILLIAM A. PEARSON.
DANIEL PECK.
FRANK PLAGGE.
GEORGE ROBERTS.
CLAUDE ROGERS.
GUS SCHALL.
PHILIP SCHNITZLER.
JOHN SCHWARTZ.
JULIUS E. SPAETH.
WILLIAM SPENCER.
JOHN SPENCER, JR.
EUGENE N. STEVENS.
FRANK M. STEVENS.
RODERICK B. STEVENS.
CHRISTOPHER THOMPSON.
ARTHUR TUERS.
CALVIN TUERS.
RICHARD K. VAN DIEN.
ALFRED WARD.
FREDERICK T. WERNICKE.
PATRICK WHITE.
WALTER D. WILLIAMS.
JAMES J. WINDLE.
JOHN ZITZOW.

COMPANY H.

OFFICERS.

FRANK E. BOYD..........Captain.
ADOLPH G. FREY.......1st Lieut.

WILLIAM H. RING......2d Lieut.
ANDREW J. HARMON...1st Sergt.
GEO. W. LAYTON.....Q. M. Sergt.
ROLAND STOLTE........Sergeant.
THOMAS F. O'BRIEN....Sergeant.
JOHN SMITH......Color Sergeant.
JAMES E. MONROE......Sergeant.
JOHN G. KNAPP..........Corporal.
FERDINAND V. FINK...Corporal.
J. T. HENDRICKSON....Corporal.
AUGUST S. HAFECR....Corporal.
HENRY A. RUMMEL....Corporal.
L. W. HIGBIE.............Corporal.
CHARLES F. COX.........Corporal.
PETER B. REILLY.......Corporal.
JOSEPH H. CURRAN....Corporal.
RALPH W. WOOD........Corporal.
J. E. OLLERENSHAW...Corporal.
HENRY J. SMALL........Corporal.
G. V. GOELERING........Artificer.
W. H. HENDRICKSON..Wagoner.
JAMES BRADLEY.......Musician.
J. H. HOWLAND.........Musician.
J. H. SHAUGER..Regime'l Bugler.
C. J. SCHULTZ..Company Bugler.

PRIVATES.

WILLIAM ARNOLD.
GEORGE D. ABER.
ARTHUR BRATHWAITE.
PERCY BRATHWAITE.
FRED W. BOCK.
EDWIN H. BALEVRE.
JAMES BRYSON.
THOMAS P. CUSICK.
JOHN J. CONNELLY.
JOHN J. COLFER.
ROBERT H. COX.
ALFRED CLOVES.
JOHN H. CAIN.
WILLIAM F. CROSBY.
JOHN P. CLINTON.
FREDERICK COOK.
WALLACE CARRAGAN.
THOMAS P. DOWD.
CHARLES DOWNS.
CORNELIUS J. DONNELLY.
CHARLES OLIVER ELLIOT.
CHARLES J. FEUERSTEIN.
JOHN FARLEY.
JAMES J. FARLEY.
JOHN P. FRANCISCO.
THOMAS H. FRANCISCO.
CHARLES FOELMLIN.
OSCAR A. GIFFORD.
HENRY J. GOELLER.
ALFRED S. GRIFFITH.
OTTO GEIGER.
JOHN GAFFNEY.
JAMES B. GARRITY.
THOMAS J. GILLIGAN.
JOSEPH GINTER.
GUSTAVE HAUFF.
JAMES B. HEALY.
JOHN J. HOEY.
CHARLES HARRIS.
THOMAS HANLEY.
IRA M. JACKSON.
FRED JAMES.
FRED J. JAEGER.
JOSEPH D. KRAMPERT.
MICHAEL KINNEY.
JOHN W. KELEHER.
JAMES KEARNEY.
CHARLES LUNN.
ALEXANDER B. LESLIE.
THEODORE S. M'NALLY.

ARTHUR R. M'NAB.
GEORGE L. MORRISS.
ALBERT E. MORRISS.
JAMES H. MAYFIELD.
WILLIAM MEEHAN.
WILLIAM D. NESTER.
FREDERICK O'HALE.
JAMES PAYNE.
WILLIAM J. ODGERS.
JAMES P. REILLEY.
CHARLES REINECKE.
GEORGE H. REED.
SAMUEL S. RODGERS.
JOHN RODGERS.
CLIFFORD S. SMITH.
JOHN J. STANTON.
JULIUS C. SEYFORTH.
JOSEPH L. SHARP.
WILLIAM E. SNOW.
WILLIAM H. SWEITZER.
HENRY SCHROEDER.
JOSEPH TROY.
JOHN TOUCHMAN.
FRED W. VREELAND.
CHARLES WAGNER.
EDWARD WOODHOUSE.
WILLIAM J. WALTERS.
PHILLIP J. WEINGARTNER.
PATRICK WARD.
HARRY WOLSEFFER.
OTTO ZEISER.

COMPANY I.

OFFICERS.

ARTHUR ROWLAND.....Captain.
FRANK L. VAN DEMAN.1st Lieut.
ARTHUR TOMALIN......2d Lieut.
ARTHUR D. MARSH....1st Sergt.
D. H. REYNOLDS......Q. M. Sergt.
J. A. KINSLEY...........Sergeant.
PAUL C. DIESING........Sergeant.
FRANK A. DE HART....Sergeant.
R. C. VANDERHOOF....Sergeant.
FRED J. KILGUS........Corporal.
WM. E. PORTER.........Corporal.
PETER P. COLEMAN...Corporal.
THOMAS D. MILLER....Corporal.
FRANK H. HAMILTON.Corporal.
PATRICK CARRAGHER.Corporal.
WM. O'GRADY............Corporal.
MICHAEL TOUEY........Corporal.
THOMAS R. CADIZ......Corporal.
JACOB J. DORST.........Corporal.
MICHAEL REYNOLDS...Corporal.
THOMAS B. M'CUE......Corporal.
ARTHUR G. TRAPPER..Musician.
HARRY N. PHILLIPS....Artificer.
JAMES R. TAGGART....Wagoner.
DAVID F. CRONK.........Clerk.

PRIVATES.

ALBERT AXT.
JOHN H. BUERCK.
ALWIN E. BORTON.
FRANCIS J. BRADY.
AUGUST BRENNECKE
EDWARD BERRY.
JOHN E. BORTON.
WILLIAM B. BAKER.
STEPHEN O. BARTLETT.
CHARLES F. CONRAD.
JOHN F. CAVANAUGH.
SIMEON D. CONNETT.

THOMAS CARROLL.
CHARLES E. CHENEVILLE.
ANDREW DE BERNARD.
AUGUST M. DAVIET.
AUGUST DIRNER.
FREDERICK DORST.
PATRICK J. DUFFY.
PHILIP H. DUFFY.
WILLIAM J. DUNN.
JOSEPH E. FLYNN.
FRED R. GALLUP.
WILLIAM F. GORDON.
WILLIAM A. GALLAGHER.
PHILIP GAHR.
JOSEPH HORTON.
ROBERT HENDRICKS.
GEORGE A. HAAS.
GEORGE E. HEWITT.
JOHN A. HASSITT.
THOMAS F. HUGHES.
FRED W. HORNER.
HERBERT A. JOHNSTON.
GEORGE G. JACOBS.
ALBERT KINGSLEY.
JOHN G. KOELSCH.
GEORGE H. KRIPS, JR.
EMIL KOLLMAR.
MIKE KINSELLA.
FREDERICK J. LANG.
ROBERT LEWIS.
WILMER D. LANTERMAN.
EDWARD M'LAUGHLIN.
EDWARD W. MARKENS.
MATTHEW M'CUTCHEON.
AUGUSTUS P. MARTIN.
JOHN MARSH.
ALBERT MEISOL.
JOHN M'ANNA.
THOMAS M'GRAIL.
CHARLES MARKEY.
JAMES MARKEY.
JAMES W. MACAULEY.
MICHAEL M'DERMOTT.
HENRY MALUVIUS.
JOHN O'GRADY.
THOMAS F. O'MARA.
GEORGE N. POST.
JOHN QUINN.
CHARLES K. REED.
JOHN C. ROBB.
WILLIAM REDMANN.
JOHN SACKMEISTER.
SIDNEY A. SYKES.
ARTHUR E. SYKES.
GEORGE SOMMERS.
JAMES SHAW.
ABRAHAM SMITH.
JOHN SCHUMAN.
JULIUS STERNBACK.
FRANK J. STULB.
JOHN F. SMITH.
FRANK O. VAN NESS.
JOHN B. VOELKER.
EDWARD M. VOIGT.
WILLIAM H. WHITTAM.
HARRY A. WYMAN.
FRED B. WURTENBURG.
CHARLES WEISER.

COMPANY K.

OFFICERS.

CORNELIUS A. REILLY..Captain.
C. ALBERT GASSER......1st Lieut.
JOSEPH B. O'ROURKE.,2d Lieut.

HARRY M'CANDLESS...1st Sergt.
WILLIAM BERGEN...Q. M. Sergt.
LAWRENCE FLYNN....Sergeant.
JOHN R. HOLMES......Sergeant.
EDWARD GORDON......Sergeant.
WALLACE E. LEE......Sergeant.
JOSEPH W. SYKES......Corporal.
JOHN D. VOGET.........Corporal.
WILBUR YORK..........Corporal.
PATRICK WHITE........Corporal.
ROBERT BOGLE.........Corporal.
EDWARD BURNS........Corporal.
JAMES FAIRHURST.....Corporal.
JOHN J. KNELL..........Corporal.
JOHN F. CARR..........Corporal.
A. CHARPENTIER.......Corporal.
FRANK M'CANDLESS...Corporal.
JOEL WILSON............Corporal.
ANDREW ASTLEY......Musician.
CHARLES BREWER....Musician.
GUS IMHOFF................Bugler.
RICHARD JACOBUS......Artificer.
G. AMMERMANN........Wagoner.

PRIVATES.

JOHN BURNS.
BERNARD BRADY.
NELSON BOWDISH.
JAMES BOLAND.
CHARLES BOUCHY.
JOHN BOOTH.
GUS L. BABBITT.
MICHAEL T. BAUDERMAN, JR.
MAX BECKMAN.
CLARENCE CHURCH.
ROBERT CLEMENS.
WILLIAM CALHOUN.
JOHN CALVEY.
JOHN C. COLEMAN.
FRANK E. CRANE.
VINCENT DUGAN.
JAMES R. DALEY.
CHARLES W. ELLIOTT.
ARTHUR W. EVANS.
AUGUST F. FREUND.
JOHN GILROY.
ALFRED GILMORE.
HARRY R. GOULD.
WILLIAM GATELY.
GUSTAV HAUG.
WILLIAM HAUG.
JOHN HOOPER.
FRED HAWTHORNE.
HARRY L. HOGEBOOM.
JOSEPH HOCH.
CHARLES HAMMOND.
FREDERICK HELLER.
PHILIPP HETTER.
ALBERT S. JONES.
THOMAS J. KANE.
GOTLIEB KREBS.
THOMAS A. KINNEY.
ANTON KOLBERG.
PATRICK LYNCH.
JAMES LOWRY.
THOMAS M'GLADE.
JOSEPH M'GOLDRICK.
JOHN M'CARDLE.
PATRICK M'GEE.
JAMES D. M'CAULEY.
GEORGE L. M'DONALD.
GEORGE M'LANEY.
JAMES F. MOFFITT.
EDWARD R. MILLER.
JOHN MURPHY.
PATRICK MURPHY

WILLIAM MURPHY.
STEPHEN MORRIS.
ALBERT C. MASON.
JOSEPH A. MINTO.
CHARLES G. E. NAER.
ROSS NEARY.
MAURICE O'HEARN.
JOHN A. O'KEEFE.
IRVING H. OLIVER.
CHARLES R. PLUM.
EDWARD Y. PURDY.
GEORGE ROLLER.
CHARLES ROBSHAW.
WALTER A. RYERSON.
JACOB STUMPF.
STEPHEN SMACK.
JOSEPH SMITH.
THOMAS J. SCANLON.
CHARLES SCOFIELD.
WILLIAM STERNKOPF.
EUGENE SHERIDAN.
HENRY STOUT.
JAMES TORNEY.
PHILIP TINDALL.
JOHN TROY.
WILSON J. VANCE.
WILLIAM H. WILSON.
THOMAS WALSH.
ARTHUR WIESSNER.
EDWARD WOLVERTON.
WILLIAM YATMAN.

MICHAEL J. CONNOLLY.
DAVID H. CRANE.
WILLIAM J. CALLAHAN.
THOMAS CASSIDY.
FRANK W. CHESHIRE.
THOMAS COSTELLO.
EDWARD CARROLTON.
HARRY CAMPBELL.
CORNELIUS N. DEENEY.
DANIEL DELANEY.
EMIL DIRGO.
WILLIAM V. DOWNEY.
CHESTER F. FITZSIMMONS.
JAMES A. FLANAGAN.
C. CLARENCE FROLEY.
AMBROSE E. FREDIRICI.
FRANK P. GORDON.
JOHN J. GEHRIG.
MICHAEL G. GRAY.
PATRICK GIVNEY.
FRANCIS W. GILHOOLY.
JAMES M. HEIMAN.
JOHN HIGEL.
JACOB HIGEL.
HARRY HOOVER.
MARTIN A. HERMAN.
GUSTAV HARTDORN.
JOHN HETRICH.
WILLIAM HAENGER.
WILLIAM HEINRICH.
CONSTANTINE J. HARVEY.
FRANK HOLGATE.
EDWARD C. KEINE.
JOHN KRUYSMAN.
JAMES A. CUBICK.
AUGUST LAIBLE.
EDWARD C. LILLY.
EDWARD A. LUNGER.
JAMES B. M'KEE.
WILLIAM R. MAUDERSCHIED.
JOHN MARTIN.
ALBERT MOORE.
WILLIAM H. MULLERY.
EDWARD MORROW.
JAMES F. MURPHY.
JOSEPH M. MOEHLER.
GAVIN S. M'MILLAN.
GEORGE C. M'COMBS.
FRANK NEUKERT.
WILLIAM NICHOLS.
GEORGE NICHOLS.
BERTRAM NIBLO.
FRANK NEWSOME.
FRANCIS OGDEN.
MICHAEL PHILBURN.
FRED PUTTBACH.
LEON SHEARS.
DANIEL SHIELDS.
WILLIAM H. SHOUP.
C. GILBERT SMITH
EDWARD SMITH.
HENRY SUTTON (Discharged.)
RICHARD STEVENS.
PETER STRECKFUSS.
HUGH SIMPSON.
JOHN SHERIDAN.
JOHN J. SKILLMAN.
CHARLES J. STIVERS.
WILLIAM J. TRACY.
WINFIELD H. VAN NEUSE.
THOMAS D. VAN SYCKEL.
HARRY S. VOORHEES.
CHARLES VAUGHAN.
FREDERICK WEGENER.
EDWIN J. WILEY.
JOSEPH WARD.
RALPH YOUNG.

COMPANY L.

OFFICERS.

THEODORE C. REISER..Captain.
LOUIS J. O'ROURKE....1st Lieut.
J. EDWARD PHILLIPS..2d Lieut.
CHARLES P. SLOAT.....1st Sergt.
WM. SCARLETT........Q. M. Sergt.
GEORGE E. THOMAS....Sergeant.
JOHN COWAN..........Sergeant.
GEORGE A. BENNETT..Sergeant.
JOS. A. FENNELLY.....Sergeant.
EDWARD E. LOUYS.....Corporal.
ARTHUR M'KINNON....Corporal.
EUGENE MORRISSEY...Corporal.
JOHN T. M'DONALD.....Corporal.
WILLIAM KENNEDY....Corporal.
THOMAS F. DEREIG....Corporal.
CHRISTIAN ZITZOW....Corporal.
THEO. FRANCISCO......Corporal.
JACOB SUTTON.........Corporal.
THOMAS D. DEVINE....Corporal.
M. HAGERSTROM.......Corporal.
WM. H. WAMBOLD......Corporal.
JOHN F. CALLAGHAN..Artificer.
FREDERICK J. HUSK..Wagoner.
ANDREW CRONIN......Musician.
JOHN J. TUERS.........Musician.

PRIVATES.

AUGUST J. BARTZ.
CHARLES E. BARR.
AUGUST E. BETSCHICK.
JOHN P. BIRMINGHAM.
FRED BREHEN.
JOHN BOEHMER.
WALTER B. CONWAY.

COMPANY M.

OFFICERS.

ED. R. WESTERVELT....Captain.
JOHN C. SCHOCH........1st Lieut.
P. J. ANDERSON.........2d Lieut.
LOUIS BUSCH............1st Sergt.
WM. J. BUSCH..........Q. M. Sergt.
RICHARD J. DREYER...Sergeant.
OTTO SPITZ..............Sergeant.
THEODORE WALZER...Sergeant.
LOUIS WIDMAN..........Sergeant.
FRED A. MILLER........Corporal.
CHARLES J. SCHWARZ.Corporal.
EDGAR A. WORK........Corporal.
EDWARD S. RILEY......Corporal.
CLARENCE H. BAILY...Corporal.
PALMER J. CHAPMAN..Corporal.
FRANK A. GILLEN......Corporal.
FRANK HIGEL...........Corporal.
A. KIESEWETTER......Corporal.
G. MERSFELDER........Corporal.
ROBERT H. CONKLIN...Corporal.
HARRY KENT............Corporal.
GUSTAV WIDMAN.......Artificer.
FRED A. WOLFE.........Wagoner.
JAMES E. M'EVOY......Musician.
JOSEPH H. GLASIER....Musician.

PRIVATES.

ISADORE ARON,
MONROE S. BERDINE.
THOMAS BLUNT.
WARREN G. BURDICK,
WILLIAM J. BARLOW.
ROBERT CROCKETT.
CHARLES A. COLLINS.
MATHEW H. COOK.
MERRITT S. CRAMER,
EDWARD J. CALLAHAN.
SIDNEY B. CURTIS.
WILLIAM A. CONGER.
ROBERT A. DICKERSON.
CHARLES E. DALEY.
CHARLES DE NICHOLS.
FREDERICK DEGLER,
CHARLES DIXON.
GUSTAVE A. ENDLICH.
JACOB A. FOEHNER,
VALENTINE GILBERT.
MARTIN GIBLIN.
JOHN W. GEISEL.
MICHAEL GARRIGAN.
JOSEPH H. GALLAGHER.
WILLIAM H. HOOD.
BERNARD HELD.
JOHN J. HALLIGAN, JR.
ROBERT HUNERBERG.
THOMAS HAFFEY.
ROBERT W. HAINES.
ANDREW J. HOFFMAN.
CHARLES JACOBI.
EDWARD KILLMURRAY.
AUGUST KASTNER.
BENJAMIN KEISER.
JOHN A. KELLEY.
TERRENCE KENNEDY.
CHARLES KNEICH.
HARRY F. LITTLE.
FRANCIS T. LOWER.
GUSTAV W. LINDEBERG.
JOSEPH LICHTENSTINE.
FRED H. MEYER.
JACOB H. MAYER.
MARTIN MILMOE.
CHARLES MILBAUER,
JOHN W. MULCAHY.
LAURENCE F. M'MAHON.
WILLIAM M'LEAN.
JOHN MOFFAT.
MICHAEL NAGLE.
HERMAN F. NAEGELE.
HERMAN F. NAGLE.
EUGENE NAGELE.
WILLIAM A. NORTON,
JAMES S. OSBORN.
ARTHUR L. ORTMAN.
ERNEST REIMULLER.
FREDERICK A. RENZ.
JOHN S. ROLLE.
FRED RUMMEL.
WILLIAM F. RUSSELL.
WILLIAM C. SIEREN.
RUDOLPH SPITZ.
GEORGE P. SAVACOOL.
CHARLES T. STEPHENS.
JAMES J. SLAIN.
HENRY SMITH.
JOHN SACHS.
CHARLES C. TRELEASE.
FRANK TALMAGE.
ALBERT T. WILLIS.
FRANK V. WILKINSON,
ALBERT B. WILLIAMS.
CHARLES H. WEAVER.
JOHN WATSON.
FREDERICK YOUNG.

THE HONORED DEAD.

WILLIAM C. CANNIFF.....Corp.
H. NELSON FRASER.
WILLIAM S. JACOBUS.
JEREMIAH MURPHY.
THOMAS J. RYAN.
WILLIAM E. SMITH.
WALTER J. SPAWN.
FREDERICK SCHWABE.
JAMES MARKEY.
NESTOR.
JOHNSON.
M'DERMIT.
ROBERT HYLAND.

SONS OF VETERANS IN FIRST REGIMENT.

Fathers of a Large Number of the Boys Fought in the Civil War, Some on the Confederate Side.

Lieutenant-Colonel R. Heber Breintnall and Major Charles B. Champlin, both of the First New Jersey Regiment of Volunteer Infantry, have had the entire command thoroughly canvassed, to obtain the names of the Sons of Veterans who are serving in the regiment. The canvass was made at the request of Major William W. Morris, city document clerk of Newark, N. J., who takes an active interest in affairs pertaining to the Grand Army.

The list includes 224 names, several of which are borne by young soldiers whose fathers wore the gray of the Confederate army during the Civil War. The list, showing the soldier's name and rank, with the name, rank and command of the father, so far as can be obtained in Camp Alger, is as follows:

Company A.

Rank and Soldier's Name.	Father's Name, Rank, Company & Regiment.
Private Frank Patterson	Henry Patterson.
Private Thomas Reilly	Michael Reilly.
Private James Fay	Patrick Fay, 2d lieut., Co. E, N. J. H'vy Art.

Company B.

First Lieutenant Herbert C. Van Houten	Cornelius Van Houten, corp., Co. B, 1st N.J.Art.
First Sergeant William H. Newman	David Newman, corp., Co. I, 29th N. J.
Quartermaster-Sergeant Herbert Jacobus	William Jacobus, private, New Jersey.
Sergeant George E. Watt	George P. Watt, sergeant, New York Cavalry.
Corporal Thomas Kersting	John F. Kersting, private, 22d N. Y. Cavalry.
Musician William Weston	Jacob H. Weston, private, Co. I, 5th N. Y. Cav.
Private Thomas Cahill	John J. Cahill, corporal, New York.
Private Daniel McCauley	Thomas McCauley, private, 9th New York.
Private Henry W. Heydecke	Charles Heydecke, private, New Jersey.
Private Joseph Brunner	Thomas Brunner, private, First New Jersey.
Private Frank Huntley	Charles Huntley, New Jersey.
Private John Hawkey	Charles Hawkey, sailor, United States Navy.
Private William J. Scott	William J. Scott, private. Co. A, First N. J.
Private Eugene Banner	William Banner, sailor, United States Navy.
Private Charles H. Robb	William A. Robb, sailor, United States Navy.
Private George H. MacDonald	James T. MacDonald, private, New Jersey.
Private Frank J. Hopkins	Michael J. Hopkins, pri., Bat. B, 1st N. J. Art.
Private Richard Burdick	Charles Burdick, private, Massachusetts Art.
Private Charles Smith	Matthew Smith, private. New Jersey Infantry.
Private Frank M. Dennis	Frank Dennis, private, New Jersey Infantry.
Private Emil Streit	Otto Streit, private, Co. B, N. Y. Vol. Infantry.
Private Charles Spicer	William S. Spicer, private, Ninth Pennsylvania.
Private William Van Wert	John Van Wert, private, 33d New Jersey Inf.
Private Cornelius V. Hall	John D. Hall, private, New Jersey.
Private Philip Longcor	John Longcor, private, Co. H, 3d New Jersey.
Private Joseph H. Longcor	John Longcor, private, Co. H, 3d New Jersey.
Private William King	Gebhardt King, private, New Jersey Cavalry.
Private Frank A. Donnelly	Patrick Donnelly, private, New York.
Private William Hayden	Wm. Hayden, sailor, pri., Co.G, Pa. In. & N'y.
Private John Gilmore	John Gilmore, private, Pennsylvania.
Private Joseph Lemon	George W. Lemon, Third Miss. Infantry, C.S.A.
Private Jacob Mauch	Jacob Mauch, Kentucky Infantry, C. S. A.

Company C.

Corporal H. Zimmerman	Jacob Stalt.
Corporal Henry Kentz	Charles Kentz, Louisiana.
Corporal Joseph Baldwin	Augustus M. Baldwin, private, 26th New York.
Wagoner William H. Barton	Robert E. Barton, private, Co. A, 1st N. J.
Private Edward Snyder	Edward Snyder.
Private William G. Campbell	W. G. Campbell, private, Co. K, 27th N. Y.
Private Charles Stevens	Roderick Stevens, private, Co. I, 31st N. J.
Private Hugh Stevens	Roderick Stevens, private, Co. I, 31st N. J.
Private Leroy S. Fales	W. D. Fales, first lieut., Co. C, 13th U. S. Reg
Private C. M. Hudson	W. H. Hudson, captain, Co. B, 5th Kentucky.
Private Joseph Kiernan	Michael Kiernan, private. New York.
Private Oscar Martin	F. Martin, private, New York.
Private L. K. Van Houten	John J. Van Houten, private, Co. B, 29th N. J.
Private Joseph Raybert	Alex. L. Raybert, private, Co. H, 3d N. J.
Private Arthur S. Ellis	John G. Ellis, sergeant, Thirteenth New Jersey.

Company D.

First Sergeant William E. Flood	Thomas Flood, private, Co. K, Eighth N. J.
Quartermaster-Sergeant Alexander W. Best	William Best, Fifth Louisiana, C. S. A.
Sergeant Walter C. Mill	J. S. Mills, New Jersey.
Sergeant Harry C. Townley, jr	Harry C. Townley, private, New Jersey.
Corporal Frank Haule	Gottlieb Haule, private, Co.F. 13th New Jersey.
Corporal Charles Krebs	Charles Krebs, private, Co. I, 3d New Jersey.
Corporal George Goetz	Wenzel Goetz, private, Co. H, 20th New York.
Artificer Harry E. Corcoran	Harry E. Corcoran, private, 69th New York.
Musician Horace J. Tichenor	James H. Tichenor, lieutenant, 100th Illinois.
Private George A. Pullis	Joseph D. Pullis, capt., Dixon's Lt. Art., N. Y.
Private Clarence E. Howell	James H. Howell, New Jersey.
Private Charles F. Danneberger	John J. Danneberger, col. sergt., Co. H, 31 N.J.
Private William H. Moore	George M. Moore, private, Co. H, 8th N. J.
Private Wilmer Munch	John J. Munch, private, New Jersey.
Private Robert Barclay, jr	Robert Barclay, private, New York.
Private George B. Honig	Charles Honig, private, New Jersey Cavalry.
Private Anson W. Leonard	E. T. Leonard, private, N. Y. Heavy Artillery.
Private Emmons H. Crump	James A. Crump, private, N. J. Heavy Art.
Private John T. Wear	Benjamin Wear, private, Seventh New Jersey.
Private Theodore F. Sowers	Noah Sowers, private, Co. B, 4th New Jersey.
Private Fred. C. Townley	Harry C. Townley, private, New Jersey.
Private Oliver H. Spencer	Sydney Spencer, corporal, New Jersey.
Private Sydney H. Spencer	Sydney Spencer, corporal, New Jersey.
Private John Davis	Tristam Davis, private, Co. I, 3d New Jersey.
Private John W. Fitzpatrick	Samuel Fitzpatrick, private, Co K, 2d N. J.
Private William E. Flood	Thomas L. Flood, private, Co. K, 8th N. J.
Private Walter H. Conner	John Conner, private, New Jersey.
Private Fred. W. Frank	Fred. W. Frank, private, Co. B, 32d N. J.
Private George Dennison	Albert E. Dennison, private, Co. A, 47th Mass.
Private Albert Schmidt	John Schmidt, private, Co. E, 39th New Jersey.

Company E.

Sergeant Peter J. Dopf	John G. Dopf, private, Co. L, 3d Regt., N. J.
Corporal Louis Dopf	John G. Dopf, private, Co. L, 3d Regt., N. J.
Corporal Joseph Huebner	———— Huebner, private, Seventh Reg., N. J.
Corporal M. H. Richardson	William T. Richardson, sergt., Pennsylvania.
Quartermaster-Sergeant William C. Schaefer	William Schaefer, private.
Private William Tronson	John F. Tronson, musician, Seventh N. J.
Private John Schlickmeyer	Joseph Schlickmeyer, private, Seventh, N. J.
Private Walter Drake	Walter Drake, private.
Private James Terwilliger	David Terwilliger, private, Co. D, 15th N. J
Private Theodore F. Hays	Harry F. Hays, private.
Private John Mertz	Frank Mertz, private.
Private James A. Pollard	Joseph Pollard, private, 69th New York.
Private John B. Brennan	John Brennan, private.
Private Thomas Bell	Thomas J. Bell, private.
Bugler John Beale	John Beale, Third New Jersey Cavalry.
Musician Royal A. Gibson	Levi E. Gibson, private.
Private William Peterson	————————, private, New York.
Private Otto Peterson	————————, private, New York.

Company F.

Corporal Lewis Nippert	Lewis Nippert, private, New Jersey.
Corporal Sherman E. White	Edwin White.
Corporal Raymond Kinney	R. W. Kinney, Sergeant, 3d N. J. Cavalry.
Musician Richard Tucker	John Tucker, gunner, United States Navy.
Bugler George A. Dixon	George Dixon, private, 21, District of Columbia.
Private William Renaud	Joseph Renaud.
Private Joseph Renaud	Joseph Renaud.
Private A. B. Clayton	James Clayton.
Private Patrick Fox	Patrick Fox, Eighth New Jersey.
Private Elmer Harris	Richard Harris, Ohio Light Artillery.
Private Fred. Morgan	John B. Morgan, corporal, 105th New York.
Private William Oberst	John Oberst.
Private Alexander E. McDougal	Albert B. McDougal, capt., 4th New York Cav.
Private Robert H. McDougal	Albert B. McDougal, capt., 4th New York Cav.
Private Joseph Clifton	John Clifton, sergeant, 40th New Jersey.
Private Cornelius Melville	Henry Melville, private.

Company G.

Corporal William Datesman	John Datesman, q't'rm'r-sergt., Co. G. 153d Pa.
Artificer Walter H. Pearson	O. R. Pearson, pri., Co. D, 6th N. J. H'y Art.
Private William A. Pearson	O. R. Pearson, pri., Co. D, 6th N. J. H'y Art.
Private Arthur Fuers	Simon Fuers, private.
Private Calvin Fuers	Simon Fuers, private.
Private Alexander Ledden	John Ledden, lieutenant.
Private Walter C. Kenann	Martin Kenann.
Private Eugene N. Stevens	Roderick B. Stevens, private, Co. I, 31st N. J.
Private Frank M. Stevens	Roderick B. Stevens, private, Co. I, 31st N. J.
Private Roderick B. Stevens, jr	Roderick B. Stevens, private, Co. I, 31st N. J.
Private John B. Norris	Jacob W. Norris, private, 71st New York.
Private Otto W. Kocher	John Kocher, musician, 7th New Jersey.
Private J. M. Conklin	M. J. Conklin, private, 12th New York.
Private Thomas Furze	W. J. Furz, sailor United States Navy.

Company H.

Sergeant Harmon	A. B. Harmon, private, 8th and 3d Penn.
Corporal Hendrickson	Charles H. Hendrickson, private.
Corporal Higbee	William L. Higbee, private, Co. H, 26th N. J.
Corporal Rummell	John Rummell, private.
Corporal Reilly	Terence Reilly, capt., brevet maj., 4th U.S.Ar
Corporal Edward Monroe	Thomas Monroe, private, Co. H, Sixth N. J.
Corporal C. Cox	———— Cox, sailor, United States Navy.
Private R. Cox	———— Cox, sailor, United States Navy.
Wagoner Hendrickson	Charles H. Hendrickson.
Private Cain	William H. Cain.
Private Tauchman	Theodore Tauchman.
Private Cook	Hugh Cook.
Private Elliott	John Elliott.
Private Colfer	James Colfer.
Private Oscar Gifford	Oscar F. Gifford, pri., Co. E, 3d R. I. Cavalry.
Private Gaffney	William Gaffney, private, Kansas Mounted Inf.

Company I.

Sergeant J. A. Kinsley	Christian Kinsley, sergt., Co. E, 3d U. S. Eng.
Corporal Frank H. Hamilton	W. Hamilton, color sergt., Co.I, Conn. Vol. Inf.
Bugler John F. Cavanaugh	F. J. Canavaugh, corporal, Co. C, 2d N. J.
Orderly John Hassitt	W. R. Hassitt, surgeon.
Artificer Harry Phillips	William Phillips, private.
Private Arthur Sykes	Thomas Sykes, private.
Private Frank Van Ness	J. H. D. Van Ness, paym'r, U.S.S. Miami, U.S.N.
Private Frederick Lang	Louis Lang, sergeant.
Private John Hobb	John R. Robb, private, Co. C, 16th Penn.
Private J. F. Smith	Michael F. Smith, private.
Private Thomas Hughes	Thos. F. Hughes, gun'r, U.S.S. Richmond, U.S.N.
Private Frederick Wurtenburger	F. B. Wurtenburger, pri., Co.I, 32d Ind.N.Y.Bat.
Private John Sackmeister	John Sackmeister, sailor, United States Navy.
Private George Post	John W. Post.
Private Sydney Sykes	Thomas Sykes.
Private David F. Cronk	Chas. W. Cronk, capt., U. S. S. Nanbric, U.S.N.
Private Charles K. Reed	S. F. Reed, private, 93d Pennsylvania.
Private George E. Sommers	G. E. Sommers.
Private Thomas O'Mara	P. O'Mara, private.
Private Thomas McGrail	J. P. McGrail, New Jersey.
Private George Haas	H. Haas.
Private Simeon D. Connett	Jonathan P. Connett, private, Co. H, 30th N. J.
Private Edward M. Voight	Ferdinand G. Voight, first lieut., 95th N. Y.
Private Albert Kinsley	Christian Kinsley, sergt., Co. E, 3d U. S. Eng.
Private Albert Axt	Gustave Axt, musician.
Private William B. Baker	John C. Baker, corporal, 14th New York.
Private Herbert A. Johnston	Jas. A. Johnston, sailor, U.S.S. Shamokin, U.S.N.

Company K.

Sergeant Wallace E. Lee	John F. Lee, sergeant, Fifth New Jersey.
Musician Andrew Astley	William Astley, Battery B, New Jersey.
Private Stephen Smack	Stephen Smack, private, Co. C, 15th N. J.
Private Gottlieb Krebs	Charles Krebs, private, 33d New Jersey.
Private George MacDonald	John W. MacDonald, private.
Private John Coleman	John H. Coleman, first lieutenant.
Private Harry Gould	Randolph Gould, private, 13th New Jersey.
Private Joseph Smith	Patrick Smith, private, 33d New Jersey.
Private Charles R. Plum	John H. Plum, private, Co. H, 1st N. J. Cav.
Private Michael J. Banderman	M. J. Banderman, private.
Private George McLancy	William McLancy, New Jersey.
Private Philip Tindall	Philip Tindall.
Private Wilson J. Vance	Wilson J. Vance, br't captain, 21st Ohio.
Private Robert Clemens	Henry Clemens, New Jersey.
Private Fred. Heller	John Heller, private, 8th New Jersey.

Company L.

Sergeant Charles P. Sloat	Edward G. Sloat, captain, Co. B, 7th N. J.
Corporal John T. McDonald	Philip McDonald, private, New York.
Corporal William Kennedy	Thomas Kennedy, private, Co. G, 2d N. J.
Corporal Thomas F. Derrig	John Derrig, private, 29th New Jersey.
Corporal Jacob Sutton	Lemuel F. Sutton, corp., Co. H, 27th N. J.
Corporal William H. Wambold	Edward H. Wambold, drummer, 8th N. J.
Wagoner Fred. J. Husk	Alfred Husk, corporal, 7th New Jersey.
Private David H. Crane	Matthias S. Crane, private, Co. E, 8th N. J.
Private William J. Callaghan	John Callaghan, private, Co. B, 1st New Jersey.
Private Thomas Cassidy	Thomas Cassily, private, Batt'r/ B, 1st N.J.Ar.
Private Clarence C. Fraley	Alfred Fraley, private, 1st N. J. Artillery.
Private Chester F. Fitzsimmons	James Fitzsimmons, private, 14th Illinois.
Private Frank P. Gordon	Stephen W. Gordon, private, 15th N. J.
Private Gustav Hartdorn	Amos Hartdorn, private, Co. G, 8th N. J.
Private James F. Murphy	John Murphy, private.
Private William R. Manderschied	Lewis P. Manderschied, landsman, U. S. N.
Private Albert Moore	William S. Moore, Bramhall's Battery.
Private Bertram Niblo	John Niblo, private.
Private George P. Nichols	William Nichols, private, 2d N. J.
Private William Nichols	William Nichols, private, 2d N. J.
Private Francis G. Ogden	Isaac G. Ogden, New York.
Private Henry M. Sutton	Lemuel F. Sutton, corporal, Co. H, 27th N. J.
Private Charles W. Vaughan	John J. Vaughan, drummer, Co. K, 155th N. Y.
Private Winfield H. Van Nuise	Chas. Van Nuise, col. sergt., Co.A, 37th N.Y.
Private Frederick Wegener	Wm. A. T. Wegener, first lieut., Co. C, 5th N.J.

Company M.

Sergeant Louis Widman	Louis Widman, private, Co. F, 39th N. J.
Wagoner Gustav Widman	Louis Widman, private, Co. F, 39th N. J.
Sergeant Otto Spitz	Frank Spitz, private, Co. D, 2d New Jersey.
Private Rudolph Spitz	Frank Spitz, private, Co. D, 2d New Jersey.
Corporal Clarence H. Bailey	Thos. L. J. Bailey, major, 17th U. S. Reg. Inf.
Private Gustave A. Endlich	Henry Endlich, private, Co. F, 39th N. J.
Private Frederick A. Renz	John M. Renz, private, 5th New Jersey.
Private Ernest Reinmiller	Louis Reinmiller, sergeant, Co. B, 40th N. Y.
Private Monroe S. Berdine	William Berdine, qu'rt'm'ter-sergt., 15th N. J.
Private Frederick Rummell	L. Rummell, corp., Co.D.1'1st Pa.; Co.F.39th N.J.
Private John A. Kelley	John Kelley, private, Co. I, 35th N. J.
Private Matthew Cook	Hugh Cook, bugler.
Private Thomas Blunt	Henry Blunt, private.
Private Frank Talmage	John Talmage, private, 15th N. J.
Private Martin Giblin	Michael Giblin.

www.ingramcontent.com/pod-product-compliance
Lightning Source LLC
Chambersburg PA
CBHW032246080426
42735CB00008B/1029